Equity Learning Communities

Equity Learning Communities

Leveraging Data to Transform Instruction in Higher Education

DANIEL L. REINHOLZ

HARVARD EDUCATION PRESS
CAMBRIDGE, MASSACHUSETTS

Paperback ISBN 978–1–68253-994-1
The Library of Congress Cataloging-in-Publication Data is on file.

Published by Harvard Education Press,
an imprint of the Harvard Education Publishing Group

Harvard Education Press
8 Story Street
Cambridge, MA 02138

Cover Design: Endpaper Studio
Cover Image: Endpaper Studio and Adobe Firefly

The typefaces in this book are Adobe Garamond Pro and Myriad Pro.

To Suparna, Manzil, and Rahi. एक दिन आ गया है |

Contents

Contents

Foreword

This insightful, well-researched book argues that data and meaningful support for teachers can come together in powerful ways that amplify equity for minoritized students. But wait: Haven't we tried this before?

In January 2002, President George W. Bush signed into law the bipartisan education reform known as the *No Child Left Behind Act* (NCLB). That same year I got my start in education, as a math teacher at an under-resourced high school in Richmond, California. At the heart of NCLB was the promise of data to make schools better and more equitable—especially schools like mine. The idea was that standardized test scores—when disaggregated by social markers like race and language proficiency—would help schools and teachers more efficiently allocate resources to the students most in need. And for a while, as a teacher of the NCLB era, I bought into that vision. But of course, it never came to pass. What went wrong?

Equity Learning Communities helps answer that complex question. One problem with the NCLB approach was that it relied on data removed from the daily work of teaching and learning. Test scores might reveal racial disparities among my Algebra 1 students, but they offered no way of connecting those inequities to my instructional decision-making. In contrast, this book shows how the right kind of data—collected with help from a classroom observation tool called EQUIP—can support teachers in learning how to build more equitable classrooms.

Now I must admit my bias here: I codesigned EQUIP with Dan Reinholz. In the fall of 2014, I had just started a tenure-track position and was thinking about what to work on next. My first call was to Dan. From years of conversation in graduate school, I knew we shared two values: (1) a deep commitment to equity and (2) a passion for building practical things that help teachers. But all I had at the time was the seed of an idea: What if teachers had a simple way of tracking the impact of their biases? What if teachers could get data on what I came to call *participatory equity*, or how fairly participation opportunities get distributed between minoritized and dominant students? For example, do Black girls, emergent multilingual students, and students with disabilities get to participate in class discussions, or is participation limited to White, able-bodied boys? Unlike test scores, this kind of data would be much closer to teachers' everyday work and thus might have a chance of moving the needle toward equity at the classroom level. It also reflects a fundamental difference in goals: collecting data to *support* people as opposed to collecting data to punish them (e.g., by threatening to fire "underperforming" teachers or to close "failing" schools).

Over the next couple years, Dan and I hashed out our methodology and built a prototype of EQUIP, which we eventually refined and released as a free, open-source web app for the education community. And over the last decade, we produced a number of empirical studies seeking to better understand the nature of inequity in classrooms. We also developed ways of supporting teachers across P–16 to make their classrooms more equitable, which Dan lays out in this book.

Together, the detailed case studies in *Equity Learning Communities* offer hope. They show that when granted adequate and useful support, teachers *can* and *do* shift their practice toward equity. We have no shortage of research documenting the many challenges facing such professional development efforts (e.g., White teachers' resistance to even talking about racism). But what we lack is research of the positive kind: quantitative and qualitative evidence of generative teacher learning for equity and substantive impact on minoritized students' classroom participation. This affirmative evidence alone represents a significant scholarly contribution.

The cases also offer several crucial lessons about what it takes to support teacher learning for equity. First, there are no quick fixes. The model of professional development presented here unfolded over the course of months. It raises the question: Why should we expect that big problems like patriarchy or ableism in classrooms can be solved in two-day, stand-alone workshops?

Second, teacher learning does not happen because of data alone—it's the people and resources (i.e., the community) we build *around* the data that facilitate changes in teachers' decision-making and instructional practice. A similar point can be made about the role of technology. A close cousin of the myth that "data will save education" is the dubious narrative that "technology will save education." What this book makes clear is that it's not about the technology per se (in this case, the EQUIP tool). Instead, it's about how coaches and instructors support each other in using technology to advance equitable teaching. It's an approach to teacher professional development that uses data and technology but ultimately centers human beings.

A final takeaway that I hope readers of this book will appreciate is just how difficult it is for a teacher to change their practice toward equity. When I read the stories in this book, I see teachers engaged in struggle—they are exemplars of what it means to "do the work." They were not forced by administrators to participate in this professional development; they volunteered because they care about equity and want to improve. But still, there isn't a straight line between realizing you hold a harmful bias and rectifying that bias. It is easy for us to say we care about equity, but it is much harder to change our teaching and change ourselves.

One of the teachers in this book spent her entire career mentoring women in mathematics. So how must she have felt when the data showed that men in her class were participating at disproportionately higher rates than women? This is emotional work. Pursuits of equity cannot be reduced to technocratic questions. *Equity Learning Communities* reveals the winding pathways teachers walk as they bravely stay engaged and work to improve their practice.

This work fits within a larger tradition of efforts to bring about educational equity and, perhaps, even educational justice. Ideally, the highest goal we can pursue is an immediate, radical transformation of society where minoritized communities are released from the weight of oppressive discourses and social systems, both in and beyond education. In reality, though, equity is often a slow, incremental, and nonlinear process. Using EQUIP or starting an equity learning community will not end White supremacy or dismantle anti-Blackness, but they can be a step in the right direction. Increasing participation opportunities means more space in classrooms for minoritized students to voice their curiosities and express their thinking. Not only does that support student learning, but it can also make a learner feel a little more human. *Equity Learning Communities* is an essential road map for educators and institutions to make equity a reality.

Niral Shah
College of Education
University of Washington, Seattle
October 2024

Preface

There is growing awareness of inequities in our education system—from racist disciplinary policies and tracking to inequities in school funding—but these problems can feel intractable. Simple solutions—like grit, mindset, or implicit bias workshops—are often proposed for complex problems. While such ideas may be beneficial when incorporated into a larger systemic change process, in isolation, they do little to improve equity on the ground.[1] One issue is a lack of consistency between instructor beliefs and practices.[2] Although instructors may espouse new beliefs after attending a workshop, these ideas don't often translate into practice. How can decades of socialization in a racist system be unlearned in a two-hour workshop?

The quest for a silver bullet contributes to conventional wisdom that "diversity trainings don't work." Empirically, diversity trainings often fail to meet their purported goals.[3] Reviews of research in inclusive education, multicultural education, and racial equity show a mixed-literature base with limited evidence, relying heavily upon instructor self-report.[4]

Overcoming historical legacies of racism, sexism, ableism, and other isms requires systemic change. Potential levers for change include policies and procedures, infrastructure, spending decisions, and human behaviors. In my experience, focusing on equity issues closest to home—in one's own classroom—is a productive starting point for addressing inequities both locally and on a larger scale. Inequities can be made salient and actionable through the effective use of data, creating a sense of *local urgency* for instructors. When instructors take up practices that reduce these patterns of inequity, it empowers them as agents of change. Effective teaching is the bedrock of quality education, but meaningful changes to teaching practice require *years* of learning.[5]

This book is not a panacea. It does not promise to revolutionize instruction or to end inequity. Nevertheless, it provides a well-documented approach to promote equitable instruction, which has been demonstrated to be effective with a variety of instructors. Instructors who follow the methods in this book will not *eliminate* inequity in their classrooms, but they are highly likely to make concrete changes that will *improve* participation by minoritized students in their classrooms and thus *reduce* inequities.

The approach I offer is called an *equity learning community*. Equity learning communities have three core features: (1) empirical data create local urgency; (2) learning communities collaboratively process the data; and (3) instructors make iterative, incremental changes to practice. The rapid pace of classroom activity often obscures dynamics that are consequential for learning and identity development. As such, many instructors remain unaware of subtle racialized and gendered classroom interactions. Data can highlight these interactions, making them actionable targets for change. While data are the foundation of the change process, not all data are equally useful. In my experience, data organized by different social-marker identities are effective at addressing classroom inequities (e.g., answering questions like, How often do Black students in my class get asked about high-level concepts?). Because classroom inequities tend to be grounded in larger identity-based systems of oppression, data must be sensitive to the diverse experiences of different groups of students. Such data make nonapparent classroom phenomena more salient, allowing instructors to teach more intentionally.

Data do not speak for themselves; instructors need support to make sense of data productively. Learning communities allow instructors to grow with their peers, building capacity for collective action. A facilitator (i.e., coach) helps the learning community process data together, and instructors come up with individual action plans. After multiple cycles of this nature, instructors transform their teaching—and sometimes, they are transformed in the process as well. Consistent, incremental changes lead to a measurable improvement in student experiences. Instructor motivation for change is enhanced when improvements are made visible through data. Students who previously seemed disengaged make meaningful contributions to class sessions, challenging preconceptions about these students. To be clear, instructional change alone is insufficient to upend deeply rooted inequities in our society, but it is a step in the right direction.

In this book, I provide an overview of equity learning communities and illustrate their impact with empirical data from six faculty case studies. The approach I describe here has continued to evolve over the years, as my research team has worked with over one hundred instructors (and other researchers have worked with many more). I hope this book allows you to continue developing this approach even further, as a tool for widespread change.

AUTHOR POSITIONALITY

My background, education, and research perspectives have all shaped the book you are reading, so I want to tell you a bit more about myself so you can understand why the book looks like it does. Equitable teaching requires a historical perspective. This work is situated in the US, which has a legacy of indigenous genocide, enslavement, xenophobia, colonialism, patriarchy, militarism, global interventionism, and other forms of oppression. To teach equitably in the US, we must confront this history. Ideas from this book are globally relevant but must be adapted for differences in culture, hierarchies of power, and historical legacies.

My identity as a White and masculine-presenting person in the US has helped me to access study and to receive advanced degrees in engineering (BS), mathematics (MS), and mathematics education (PhD). Since college instructors are disproportionately White and male, my conviction is that we have a responsibility for addressing historical inequities that persist today, given our collective role in perpetuating such inequities. I have dedicated my career to working with other instructors (especially those who are White) as a means of harm reduction and to make learning more equitable, inclusive, useful, and joyful for everyone.

Despite my current levels of professional success, I am a first-generation college student and high school dropout. I am a parent of two young children, and the adventure of being with two beautiful, young humans has profoundly shaped who I am. I am autistic, nonbinary, and disabled, living with chronic illness since birth. These identities are largely nonapparent to people who do not know me or do not know how to see them. They shape my viewpoint and experience of the world, and they shape the book I have written. For example, my experience organizing learning communities, my approach to analyzing data, and my interactions with others while doing equity work all are influenced by these identities. Individuals with other identities will likely have different experiences based on their own viewpoints and how the world sees them differently. When I write about the coaching process, I address these identities directly.

I cannot speak from intersections of identities other than my own, but broadly speaking, this work has been informed by the perspectives of many others who have different identities and lived experiences from me. Moreover, as an instructor, I have worked across a variety of settings, including K–12 schools, community colleges, universities, and San Quentin State Prison. This has informed my view of education in many contexts. I recognize the inherent limitations of a single author writing a book and have done my best to represent the wisdom and viewpoints of many colleagues and collaborators.

Introduction

Higher education does not exist in a vacuum; it is subject to societal forces, changes, and trends. Movements like Black Lives Matter, Occupy Wall Street, Me Too, disability justice, marriage equality, and climate justice have brought social justice to the forefront of the discourse in the US. And in an era dominated by social media bubbles and targeted advertising, the US is more polarized than ever. Controversies and division often play out in education, from the Common Core and math culture wars to far-right speakers inciting angst on college campuses, pitting *free speech* against *social justice*. Given this context, ongoing impacts from the global COVID-19 pandemic, and increasing economic inequities, the challenges for equity on college campuses are as pressing as they have ever been in recent history. However, we live in a time in the US where it is easier to talk about equity than to enact it.

In the wake of protests for the racial justice movement and a shift to online teaching during a global pandemic, there has been a resurgence of support for equitable teaching.[1] Campuses have generated awareness through invited speakers, lectures, discussions, and book clubs. *Equity talk* is flourishing (whether *for* or *against* equity). Terms like *implicit bias*, *intersectionality*, *microaggressions*, *white supremacy*, and *critical race theory* are now commonplace, no longer hidden in academic articles. In my own professional work, I have been encouraged by this increased awareness. But awareness is not change. I find that many instructors want to do *something* but don't know what to do. *It's much easier to talk about equity than to enact it.*

Let me be frank about the realities of faculty life. Our job as instructors plays an important role in shaping the future of our society, but this work is woefully underappreciated and underfunded. Our teaching must be balanced with the many responsibilities of our energetic professional lives. For research faculty with pressure to secure external funding, publish in top-tier journals, and develop an international reputation, teaching often takes a back seat. For teaching faculty, high course loads limit their ability to know their students as individuals. Yet research shows that the relationships students develop with faculty mentors and the experiences that students have in the classroom are some of the most important facets of the college experience that shape their learning and persistence.[2] Equitable teaching is one practical avenue for instructors to enact equity. I have spent the past decade developing *equity learning communities* to create measurable improvements in teaching, while honoring instructors' time constraints. To be clear, better teaching will not upend systemic racism, sexism, and ableism in our society. But better teaching does reduce the everyday harm that minoritized students experience in today's classrooms. It also provides a foundation for larger systemic change efforts.

Historically, the concept of "academic freedom" has been used to position college teaching as a personal, private act that is entirely up to the discretion of individual instructors.[3] Consequently, instructors received less mentoring around teaching than research, which is public and connected to the prestige of an institution. Paradoxically, instructors can be leading experts in their disciplines but still developing the skills required to effectively teach the discipline to others. This has started to shift over time, and many academics begin to receive pedagogical training as graduate students, which is continued by other professional-learning programs on campuses. Instructors may learn from one-off workshops, online modules, lunch and learns, or ongoing learning communities, but these opportunities are not equally conducive to learning.

After decades of research, our field has a much clearer picture about how people learn. The same principles of classroom learning can support instructors too. Just like how learning to ride a bike requires getting on the bike and trying to figure out how to balance, learning to teach better requires implementing new practices, receiving feedback, reflecting on those practices, and trying to iteratively improve one's implementation. Effective professional learning is embedded in the professional work of teaching, and it must be ongoing and long-term.[4] While one-and-done workshops can build awareness, they rarely lead to meaningful changes in instruction when conducted in isolation. It's like watching a movie trailer and then skipping the film. It's enticing but short-lived. In this chapter, I provide an overview of how people learn and the ways that inequities can arise in learning environments.

HOW PEOPLE LEARN

Active learning has become a buzzword in higher education, describing classroom experiences that involve students in the learning process (e.g., by creating models, solving problems, discussing with peers, critiquing the work of others).[5] Extensive research documents how active-learning environments are better aligned with human-learning processes than pure lecture.[6] To be clear, active learning doesn't mean that instructors *never* lecture; it means that they do not *only* lecture.

Active learning isn't a new idea. Nearly a hundred years ago the educator John Dewey advocated for learning through authentic practices.[7] He believed that if children are to take on certain roles as adults through different professions, then the learning process in schools should reflect the actual lived realities of those professionals and their practices. Long before Dewey, cultures around the world used apprenticeship to teach skills and trades like hunting, foraging, cooking, and navigation. As anyone who spends a lot of time with children knows, activities like learning to walk, using a spoon, having a conversation, or preparing food are modeled for children who then engage at a level appropriate to their ability. I've never met a child who learned to use a spoon through pure lecture.

Why, then, is lecture the predominant pedagogical model in universities? It is a historical vestige of a time before books were widely available or affordable, and thus, sharing technical knowledge was a key function of education.[8] Historically, lecture made sense as a primary way to engage with students, efficiently transmitting information to a lot of people. (Whether or not the people receiving that information understood it, however, is another question altogether.) Today, we live in an era of information, with e-books and online platforms such as ChatGPT, YouTube, Instagram, and TikTok. Lecture is no longer the only or best way to access disciplinary knowledge.

The proliferation of access to information could be a catalyst that fundamentally transforms teaching and learning. Imagine the time that instructors could use to meaningfully engage our students and provide feedback now that we no longer need to deliver all the content to our students in a lecture. Why is it, then, that education looks largely the same as it did decades ago? As it turns out, developing effective pedagogical practices is not easy, so most of us adopt the pedagogies used by those before us.[9] Learning to authentically engage students requires instructors to develop an extensive amount of new pedagogical expertise, often while balancing the immense pressures of research productivity and faculty life, which disincentivizes change. These institutional and cultural pressures are effective at perpetuating the dominance of lecture, despite research showing that purely lecture-based environments can alienate students and deter them from continuing in their majors, especially in STEM fields.[10]

In my own field of mathematics education, there is a long and highly politicized history of debate between active and lecture-based teaching methods.[11] After all, today's most skilled mathematicians learned primarily through traditional methods. It's also true that—partially due to the proliferation of those traditional methods—there is a perception in the US that some people simply aren't "math people."[12] Relative to its positionality as a global superpower, the US education system has struggled to produce a mathematically literate populace compared to global peers,[13] which has spurred renewed and ongoing interest in this topic. This interest is often driven by the connections between STEM fields, economic prosperity, and international competitiveness.[14] Over time, although some are still in vehement opposition, there has been a growing consensus from leaders in the mathematics community that there is a need to foster active learning. For example, a recent statement was signed by the leadership of nearly every major mathematical organization in the US calling for "mathematics departments" to "invest time and resources to ensure that effective active learning is incorporated into post-secondary mathematics classrooms."[15]

LEARNING AS A CULTURAL PROCESS

Active learning works because learning is a cultural process.[16] The sociocultural paradigm has transformed how educators think about learning, with a specific emphasis on how learning is situated within social contexts. Our abilities to learn and develop new skills, use language, and create tools to serve our needs are all core parts of what it means to be human. As humans, we perpetuate our collective learning through the transmission of culture. Thus, fundamentally, we can view learning as a process of enculturation.

Consider two examples from the discipline of mathematics. As young children learn to understand numbers, fingers are commonly used to represent quantity.

Within any given cultural context, most people will count on their fingers in the same way, and this is taken for granted as "the way" that finger counting happens. Yet, across the world and throughout history, there has been remarkable diversity in finger counting.[17] In the US, I learned to assign one number to each finger, allowing me to count to ten using both hands. In India, my partner learned to assign numbers to each *digit* of the finger using the thumb as a pointer and counting to twelve on one hand. In ancient Babylon, they counted the same way on the right hand, using each finger on the left hand to complete a cycle of twelve on the right (the astute reader may realize that this allows one to represent $5 \times 12 = 60$ on the hands, which leads to a base-60 system and forms the basis of how we partition time). The use of our fingers plays a fundamental role in conceptualizing numbers, and how we use our fingers depends on our enculturation.

As another example, consider the abacus. The abacus was developed in early history as a tool to facilitate computation. It is no longer used in most parts of the world, but the *soroban* (Japanese abacus) is still commonly used in Japan. Beyond facilitating computation, the abacus fundamentally shifts how one conceptualizes arithmetic. In fact, through proper training, one can internalize a visual representation of the abacus (a mental abacus) and perform arithmetic feats like mentally multiplying three-digit numbers or adding numbers in the trillions.[18] This isn't a more efficient way to use standard addition algorithms; it is a fundamentally different way of approaching arithmetic. Cultural artifacts are not merely aids to support learning; they provide a foundation for higher-level cognition.

Other examples abound. In countries (other than the US) where the metric system is used in everyday life, students have a more intuitive sense of the units of measure used in the sciences.[19] The sounds that children hear as babies (e.g., different sounds or accents in different languages) shape which sounds the brain is attuned to, making it nearly impossible to achieve the same status as a native language speaker when learning a new language as an adult.[20] Different languages have different words and concepts with them, and in fact, language is so powerful, that the primary language we learn can shape the way that we see the world.[21] In countries where children are surrounded by many languages, they are better able to pick up new languages, compared to monolinguals.[22] Playing music—a core element of culture—also changes the brain, influencing emotion and cognition.[23] Such learning is iterative, consisting of cycles of instruction, feedback, and a healthy dose of practice. This learning is embodied and is mediated by artifacts, peers, teachers, society, and culture.

A long line of theorization has helped us understand the learning process, owing to foundational contributions from scholars like Vygotsky, Lave and Wenger, and many others.[24] This work compels us to abandon unexamined assumptions of lecture-driven models of education. Enculturation happens through participation in practices with others. (Even when we learn "by ourselves," sociocultural processes dictate everything from how we perceive objects to the way we use our bodies.) Humans are social beings. We learn to be human by being with others. These interactions teach us which behaviors are socially acceptable. Yet, there is not a single "human culture," and people of various backgrounds have different experiences of socialization. Furthermore, due to our social-marker identities (race, gender, etc.), different people will be treated differently in the same context. Children at a very young age are taught gender roles and other basic assumptions about people given their social-marker identities, even though these assumptions are not always true. Assumptions help simplify our complex world to facilitate decision-making, but overgeneralizations of assumptions can also lead to misunderstandings and harm.

Equity learning communities are fundamentally grounded in this sociocultural view of learning. Rather than indirectly learning about equity (through a lecture or book club), participating instructors are given data alongside concrete opportunities to enact equitable teaching practices. This practical apprenticeship is an experience of enculturation into a new way of teaching. Furthermore, participants who later serve as coaches learn much about coaching from how their prior coaches interacted with them. Thus, even though this book provides a wealth of information about equity learning communities, it is only a starting point. To truly understand this work, you must enact it in your own context, collecting data, getting feedback, and iteratively improving along the way. To understand a culture, we can't just read about it, we must live it. Similarly, to learn anything of consequence, we can't just read about, but we must enact it.

PROFESSIONAL LEARNING THROUGH COMMUNITIES

Although professional learning has been studied for decades, there are still limited rigorous research studies documenting a positive impact on students.[25] Out of these promising approaches, essentially none have been scaled reliably across contexts and facilitators.[26] Lack of funding for rigorous educational research and the challenges of professional development are major barriers to overcome.[27] There is an urgent need for effective, reliable, and scalable models of change. Challenges aside, effective professional learning is long-term (ideally a year or more), sustained, and ongoing.[28]

Learning communities are a common approach that meet the above criteria. Given that learning is fundamentally a social process, it should be unsurprising that learning communities have become a popular approach to professional development. Learning communities involve instructors as active participants in a collective space for a sustained amount of time, which are all features related to effective coaching.[29] The community allows a coach (or facilitator) to leverage the social space in a way that supports ongoing collective learning that differs from one-on-one coaching. Meaningful relationships allow for communities to persist over time and continue to evolve.

Theoretically, the concept of a *community of practice* can help us better understand how learning communities work.[30] A community of practice can be understood as a group of people who either share a common interest or are part of the same profession. As a community, people come together to share their experiences, learn from each other, and engage in dialogue about their specific practice. Interactions may occur in a variety of settings, from the workplace to a community center, or even virtually on a mailing list or message board. A community of practice may develop a common lexicon; sets of stories, myths, or key figures; or a set of shared values.

For example, experimental physicists share knowledge with each other formally through journal publications, gathering at conferences, and other correspondences. This community values empirical work and has developed a set of techniques for engaging in more rigorous experimental studies. This group tends to know a lot about physics and may even use physics language to talk about everyday social phenomena (e.g., *feedback loops*, *activation energy*, or *quantum entanglement*).

More informally, gamers could constitute a community of practice. These people meet in places like gaming shops or online message boards. Shared values constitute strategic thinking and possibly competition (depending on the types of games people like). Gamers share updates with one another about new games that are coming out. There are even stereotypes in broader society about the types of people who like to play board games and video games.

Within a community of practice, both individual and collective learning take place. For example, a new experimental technology developed by a single research team could proliferate to influence the entire field of experimental physics. Similarly, the internet has shifted how people think about tabletop gaming and who might engage in it. Card games that once used physical cards may now be represented electronically. Overall, the community may learn and share new ideas as a part of historical and cultural development. At an individual level, particular community members may learn more from each other as they become increasingly central to the community. The phrase *legitimate peripheral participant* refers to members at the margins of a community who are just learning a practice and may not yet engage the same way an expert does.[31] Over time, a new member may become increasingly central to the group. Alongside the learning process, then, there is a process of becoming, often referred to as identity development. Through this process, an individual begins to see themselves as a part of the community and is more likely to be identified that way by others.

As with all things human, power, privilege, and politics manifest within communities of practice. Higher-status individuals in the community experience benefits associated with popularity and influence, where their contributions are valued above others, and they have more potential to shape the directions of the community. Status is often connected to specific social-marker groups. For example, both physics and gaming have a history of excluding women and other minoritized groups (e.g., the GamerGate scandal in video game journalism). When we connect membership within communities to social-marker identities, it becomes clear that not all people have equal access to belonging, identity, and growth in each community of practice. This is true within both classroom environments and learning communities that we create with instructors.

A professional learning community is typically convened as a temporary group that aims to achieve a specific goal (e.g., curricular change, improved instruction). Within a team, learning happens at both individual and community levels. Because members of the community learn from their peers, the overall composition of a group can have a large impact on the personal benefits the members receive. As a result, a careful choice of team membership is a major factor for its overall efficacy.

Learning communities are more efficient when they have a skilled facilitator. Although it requires resources to have a facilitator, this also enhances how much each participant learns from the process, so it is typically a good investment of resources. (While beneficial, a facilitator is not a prerequisite for starting a learning community.) In general, a learning community meets regularly (at least once a month) for a substantial period (ideally a year or more). In a way, a professional learning community becomes a temporary and ad hoc community of practice, designed to support the professionalization of its membership. There are many possible configurations for professional learning communities, but the literature is not expansive enough to identify an ideal structure.

One feature of a professional learning community that is particularly relevant to my work is the use of data. Data take on many forms—including prior grades, diagnostic assessments, student surveys, and classroom observations—and can be used to support changes to instruction. Broadly speaking, instructors are more likely to use data when they perceive it as directly relevant to instruction.[32] Critically, data do not speak for themselves, and coaches (and learning communities more broadly) shape how instructors use their data.[33] Coaches can support instructors in making connections between the data and actionable next steps.[34] Such supports enhance the ability of instructors to use data meaningfully. In the next chapter, I outline an *equity learning community*, the type of professional learning community this book focuses on. First, I explore what is known about equitable participation (or lack thereof) in classroom activity.

STUDENT LEARNING THROUGH EQUITABLE PARTICIPATION

More people in education are talking about equity than ever before. But what exactly does equity mean? As a term, *equity* is so broad that it is easy to get a large set of stakeholders on board with the mission of "improving equity," yet simultaneously, the stakeholders may have very different ideas about what their actual goal is (e.g., is it racial diversity, economic competitiveness, or political freedom?). If these stakeholders were to discuss specific goals, they might not agree at all. Personally, while I believe goal alignment is valuable, lofty conversations can also impede changing practice on the ground. In a capitalist society, any equity goals will be couched within an institution's profit motive. This explains why the best-funded equity initiatives are aligned with the politics of the time.

On college campuses today, equity tends to focus on improving graduation rates for different populations (e.g., based on race, first-generation students, socioeconomic status). This aligns with profit motives, as student attrition costs universities *billions* of dollars annually.[35] Administrators implement a variety of strategies, from scholarship programs to summer bridge programs, supplemental instruction, cohort programs, tutoring centers, and identity-based cultural centers. These initiatives are framed as equity initiatives, with the primary goal being to increase student success for students from minoritized groups. These strategies typically complement efforts to improve teaching. Clearly, changes are needed inside and outside the classroom to address deep-rooted inequities on college campuses. In this book, my focus is classroom teaching.

Equity learning communities are a practical approach to equity, focused on immediate action and harm reduction. While broader systemic changes are clearly needed to create a more just society, such change takes a very long time. Moreover, lofty equity conversations can impede change when perfection becomes the enemy of progress. A practical starting point is instruction because it is within the direct locus of control of instructors.[36]

Specifically, I focus on *participatory equity*, which concerns the fair distribution and uptake of learning opportunities across students.[37] When students actively participate in disciplinary practices, it supports their learning. Empirical research documents multiple reasons why participation supports learning.[38] First, when students actively construct their understandings—for example, by explaining concepts—it helps them consolidate their thinking to develop more robust conceptions.[39] Second, students can receive feedback on their emergent ideas.[40] Third, participation supports positive identity development.[41]

Yet a wealth of research—including many studies by my team—shows that classroom-participation opportunities are often unfairly distributed.[42] From a social perspective on learning, this means that opportunities to learn are not fairly distributed within the classroom. Non-minoritized students tend to take up a disproportionate number of participation opportunities in active-learning classrooms. As a result, they benefit more than their minoritized peers, and thus active learning can be detrimental to equity.[43]

What constitutes fair participation, though? Defining the "ideal" distribution of participation, especially as an outside observer, seems fraught. Instead, Niral Shah and I have leveraged the concept of equality as a waypoint toward equity.[44]

Given that minoritized students tend to receive less than a proportional share of opportunities, from this baseline, reaching equality would be a clear improvement. However, to account for historical injustices in education, equity likely requires that historically minoritized students receive *more* than an equal share of participation opportunities. While a definition of equitable participation is elusive, inequity is defined as any distribution of participation that affords less than a proportional set of learning opportunities to minoritized learners. Empirically, my team and I have observed hundreds of classrooms with inequitable distributions of student participation, and never once have we entered a classroom that appeared *equitable* without an instructor reflecting on their data and making concrete changes to practice.

WHY IS PARTICIPATION INEQUITABLE?

Once one understands how inequities operate, it would be *surprising* if classroom participation were in fact equitable. Classroom dynamics mirror an inequitable society. Moreover, power dynamics within fields such as mathematics, physics, history, or art influence students aspiring to join such communities. Yet, as already discussed, not all students have equal access to participation within a discipline. Stereotypes position some students as belonging (or not) due to their race, gender, or disability. Stereotypes are not simply immaterial ideas, but they manifest with material consequences that negatively impact minoritized students.

For example, who gets to participate—and thus learn—in the classroom is often mediated by stereotypes.[45] This creates a status quo where White boys and men are disproportionately represented as participants in many classroom spaces in the US.[46] Similarly, minoritized students are more likely to experience microaggressions.[47] Moreover, as a result of stereotypes, teachers tend to hold lower expectations for minoritized students and provide them with lower-quality opportunities to learn.[48] Stereotypes also lead to stereotype threats—stressors created by a high-pressure situation in which students fear that their performance would confirm a negative stereotype about them—inhibiting the performance of minoritized students in high-stakes testing situations.[49] Stereotypes also impact racial disparities in discipline, as certain behaviors are interpreted in disproportionately negative ways for students of color.[50] Taken together, all these mechanisms play out in ways that limit opportunities for minoritized students and reify inequity.

These inequities have been studied for decades and are relatively well understood. One line of research that is particularly helpful for understanding and disrupting such hierarchies is *Complex Instruction*, which is organized around the sociological construct of status.[51] *Status* refers to how a student is perceived in a local environment and the weight that is given to their contributions (i.e., the contributions of high-status students tend to be more highly valued). Specifically, my work has drawn from the strategy of *assigning competence*, which features in the case studies of both Anne and Sam in later chapters. To assign competence, an instructor must (1) identify a low-status student, (2) identify a contribution from that student, and (3) make the importance of the contribution public. In doing so, the instructor positions the student positively and elevates their status to their peers. This has the effect of elevating future participation in the classroom from that student. Over time, the effect of assigning competence is to redress the status hierarchies that are created by negative stereotypes and thus create a more equitable learning environment.

WHAT IS THE EMPIRICAL EVIDENCE FOR PARTICIPATORY INEQUITY?

Niral Shah and I have spent the last decade studying classroom inequities across hundreds of classrooms. Our work demonstrates that inequity is ubiquitous and predicable. Students from dominant groups tend to dominate, and minoritized students are relegated to more peripheral positions in the classroom. While this is not true in *all* circumstances, this is a general trend that is remarkably robust at reproducing itself across contexts.[52] The reason is simple. Classrooms are embedded in a larger inequitable society, and the inequities from that larger society reproduce themselves in the classroom.

The most extensive study I have conducted focused on middle school mathematics instruction across a large racially diverse school district.[53] The study was a secondary analysis of existing data from the MIST project led by Paul Cobb and others at Vanderbilt. This was a professional-development study across four districts. We chose to analyze one specific district because it was the most instructionally advanced of the four districts (according to a variety of metrics developed in the initial project). We analyzed teaching across one hundred middle school classrooms, captured over a period of four years. Observations consisted of video records of two sequential lessons (about one hundred minutes total). Student demographic information was collected by the original project team. We used hierarchical linear modeling to link participation to race and gender across classrooms.

The findings were striking and emblematic of inequities across settings. On average, boys contributed 2.10 times (during their two-lesson unit), which was significantly greater than the 1.72 times for girls.[54] Gender differences were most significant when boys contributed *without being called on* by the instructor by just shouting out an answer. There were also racial inequities. White and Black students (1.80 and 1.92 contributions on average, respectively) had significantly more contributions than Asian / Pacific Islander and Latine students (1.17 and 1.14 contributions on average, respectively).[55] This means that an average White student would contribute about 58 percent more often than an average Latine student in this district.

Although these average differences in participation appear small, their cumulative effect over time has a large impact. Consider the gender gap between boys and girls (0.38 contributions on average). When this difference is aggregated over the dataset, it amounts to 379 *more* contributions from boys than girls. Given the robustness of such patterns across contexts, when we consider such a pattern repeated year after year in mathematics classrooms, it contributes to a male gender bias in math. In fact, every single study we have conducted in mathematics classrooms has revealed gender inequities, and these inequities tend to be *larger* in higher education.[56] Studies in other disciplines have been largely concordant with these results, with the largest inequities in favor of boys and men appearing in the most masculine-stereotyped STEM disciplines (e.g., math and engineering versus public health).[57] These findings are largely consistent with prior work showing how girls receive fewer meaningful participation and learning opportunities in K–12 schools.[58]

We have also studied racial inequity across a wide variety of classrooms.[59] A consistent finding is that White and (some but not all) Asian students tend to have ample participation opportunities across settings.[60] One challenge of summarizing the studies is that racial demographics are not static but are context based.

Our studies have looked at a variety of other social markers, but less systematically. In a study of multimodal instruction and disability, we found that instructors were effective at increasing multimodal teaching, but that did not necessarily translate to opportunities for disabled students.[61] Other social markers we have studied include socioeconomic status, first-generation status, major, religion, and small-group membership. In general, as one would suspect, the more axes along which a student is privileged, the more likely they are to participate.

This finding is robust and consistent across hundreds of settings in a variety of disciplines and grade levels. As will be evident later in the book, every single instructor who participated initially had inequities in their classroom participation, which they learned to reduce through instructional change.[62]

Other studies have focused on small-group instruction.[63] In brief, while we found that minoritized students typically had more opportunities to participate in the small groups, there were also problematic microaggressions in those settings. Thus, while small-group engagement can be a useful way to provide participation opportunities and vary the instructional approach, it is not without pitfalls that need to be addressed.

BRINGING IT ALL TOGETHER: TOWARD EQUITY LEARNING COMMUNITIES

This introduction presented key concepts about learning, participation, and equity. This research describes learning as a quintessentially social and cultural process, taking place in conjunction with language, tools, and other people. Unavoidably, power dynamics manifest in social spaces. These concepts apply to the work of individual instructors and to the process of supporting instructor learning. Bringing these ideas together, my team has created the equity learning community approach to supporting instructor development. This is a specific type of professional learning community that uses data to address participatory inequities in the classroom through iterative changes to practice. Equity learning communities are ongoing, sustained, and tied to practice, which is consistent with best practices for professional learning.[64]

These cases document the role of data, community learning, and incremental change. Because data are central to the process, I can track the causal impacts of the professional-learning opportunities to instructional change. Having read through this book, you'll have the background to begin experimenting with equity learning communities in your own context.

In the first chapter, I describe the equity learning community approach: structures, typical learning trajectories, and common pitfalls. The next four chapters illustrate instructor learning, each with a different theme. Chapter 2 demonstrates how small incremental changes can accumulate into a large impact on students. Chapter 3 traces how an instructor's conceptions of equity can shift throughout their participation in a learning community. Chapter 4 illustrates longitudinal change over time, tracking two participations for multiple years.

Chapter 5 shows how former participants can leverage their experiences to become effective coaches. Taken together, the case-study chapters provide an in-depth look at the processes of equity learning community involvement and a wealth of practical wisdom that an instructional coach could apply to their own work. Chapter 6 culminates insights and guides administrators and change agents to use this approach in their own contexts. Appendix A is about methodology. It provides fine-grain details of the research program, from coding to data analysis. I also provide example protocols that we used in the instructor interviews.

This book draws upon work that took place from fall 2018 to fall 2022. Over this four-year period, my team systematically collected data from twenty-one participants, including over fifty interviews, more than fifty learning-community meetings, hundreds of classroom observations, and countless hours of data analysis. This work is a subset of the larger sample of over one hundred instructors we have worked with across projects.

Throughout the four-year process, much was learned about how to create a productive equity learning community. This book is the culmination of everything we discovered over that time. For most readers, this book was written to be read straight through. For researchers, it may be helpful to first read chapter 1, "Equity Learning Communities," skip to appendix A, "Methods," and then later read the case studies. For someone looking to quickly skim through this book, reading chapter 1, "Equity Learning Communities" and chapter 6, "Bringing It All Together" is the quickest route to the key findings.

CHAPTER 1

Equity Learning Communities

This chapter provides an overview of equity learning communities. There are three core features of an equity learning community: (1) empirical data create local urgency; (2) learning communities collaboratively process the data; and (3) instructors make iterative, incremental changes to practice. The chapter begins with a discussion of practical measures of equity, which are tools for generating timely and actionable data to address classroom inequities. I discuss the process of choosing a measure, collecting data, and fostering reflection on those data through community. Coaches and participants can utilize any practical measure that attends to equity; the data in this book were generated with the EQUIP methodology, which I codeveloped with Niral Shah.[1]

The remainder of this chapter focuses on the collaborative-learning process for incremental instructional change. Communities begin with an intake interview process so that coaches can start building relationships. These intake interviews also allow coaches and participants to collectively determine the types of data that they would like to collect and for what purpose. These data are then integrated into an iterative reflection process, including (1) collecting or observing data, (2) analyzing the data, (3) providing feedback and debriefing, and (4) making incremental changes to practice. Together, these components constitute a reflection cycle. As participants complete multiple cycles, they make measurable improvements to their teaching.

Instructors may learn at different rates, and instructors may go through cycles of progress and regression as they revise their teaching practices. The goal is not for all instructors to reach the same end point but for all instructors to make progress. Experience and prior knowledge dictate an instructor's readiness to take up new equitable teaching strategies. Participants who are motivated to improve equity but lack concrete strategies are ideal candidates for an equity learning community. I also discuss common pitfalls and ways to overcome them. This chapter will serve as a vital reference for anyone who wishes to build their own equity learning community.

MEASURING EQUITY

Over the past decade, Niral Shah and I have developed practical measures of equity—metrics (often quantitative) that are easy to deploy to support instructional change. Our research explicates how data can support difficult conversations (e.g., about racism in the classroom). As described in the previous chapter, we attend to participatory equity because participation is foundational to learning and tends to be inequitable. Moreover, through the uptake of specific strategies, changing participation patterns is within an instructor's locus of control. A key feature of participation data (e.g., as compared to student assessments) is their timeliness, which allows instructors to make iterative changes that are consequential for improving student experiences.

Our measurement approach generates participation metrics that are low inference, relatively objective, and directly actionable. To create nonjudgmental metrics, we do not define "ideal" practice (e.g., by rating instruction on a one-to-five equity rubric). Our experience is that nonjudgmental data provide a foundation for vulnerable conversations. In contrast, scaled rubrics are inherently evaluative. Even if rubrics are framed as nonjudgmental, a rating of five is commonly understood as better than a rating of one. Judgment spurs defensiveness—due to the social desirability of being seen as a "good person"—which inhibits change.

Our work has been driven by questions like, How do we characterize inequitable classroom participation? Which types of data are most consequential to practice? How do we support instructors to effectively use data? To answer these questions, we first needed to develop a method to reliably generate equity metrics and, second, to study the learning processes associated with such data. Here I describe how data are generated, and throughout the chapter, I describe the equity learning community process (i.e., a mechanism for learning).

To be clear, quantitative metrics have limitations. Consequently, we use a mixed-methods approach that also includes interviews, surveys, and other qualitative measures. Although quantitative metrics have utility in shaping practice, they are not a substitute for students' subjective feelings or learning outcomes. Reflections on data analytics should be expansive enough to include these issues as well.

THE EQUIP METHODOLOGY

To streamline the process of generating quantitative metrics of participatory equity, Niral Shah and I developed the *EQUIP (Equity QUantified in Participation) methodology.*[2] More than an observation tool, EQUIP provides a fundamentally different approach to observing classroom equity. Our specific focus is on classroom conversations as being a key site within which inequities manifest. Existing tools focus almost exclusively on classroom practice writ large without attending to individual students or groups of students.[3] Such tools describe *what* happens in the classroom but fail to answer *who* questions, such as:

- *Who gets to participate?*
- *Whose ideas are central to the discussion?*
- *Who is being marginalized?*

Empirically, research shows that classroom inequities are grounded in social-marker identities. Accordingly, observation tools should also attend to these identities. We call this characteristic of equity metrics *social-marker specificity.* By failing to disaggregate participation, most classroom-observation tools fail to redress inequities. They implicitly assume that all students experience the classroom in the same way. This was true when we began our work nearly a decade ago, and it is mostly true today. There is a dearth of tools to capture classroom equity.

Why does social-marker specificity matter?

Having worked with a wide range of instructors, we have noticed that many people—especially White people—have an aversion to talking about race.[4] Even when racialized patterns are evident, people are inclined to offer alternative explanations. Instructors commonly focus on innate student traits—slow, fast, lazy, privileged, strong, weak, and so forth—ignoring systemic oppression. Similarly, instructors may classify women as shy or disabled students as unreliable. This focus on individual attributes ignores social context.[5] From this perspective, equity work is about enhancing support for students with so-called weak preparation. This deficit lens positions minoritized students negatively and obscures their strengths. It's easier to build on what students have rather than what they lack.

People more readily identify inequities related to their lived experiences. Instructors of color are more likely to notice racialized phenomena than White instructors. Women are more likely to identify sexism than men. Personally, as a disabled person, I am more attuned to the subtle ways that ableism plays out in everyday interactions. Thus, given our own individual biases, having social-marker data helps us see other forms of inequity.

Social-marker specificity transcends "equity for all" by concretely grounding classroom disparities in larger systems of oppression. Equity metrics in the EQUIP methodology have social markers baked in by design to encourage conversations about social markers (e.g., how race is connected to amounts of participation). This specificity is necessary to move beyond general equity talk to instructional change. By processing data alongside instructors, a coach gains insight into instructor ideologies, based on their interpretations of the data (e.g., do they miss a clearly gendered interaction?). These insights can be used to chart a course for instructor learning.

Unit of analysis

To operationalize social-marker specificity, the primary classroom event of interest (i.e., unit of analysis) in the EQUIP methodology is a *student contribution*. A single contribution constitutes all participation from an individual student that is not interrupted by another student.[6] By segmenting classroom practice into discrete contributions, any time a teacher or student action is coded it is associated with a specific student. This allows us to generate a profile of interactions for each individual student in a classroom. By incorporating student demographic information, we can aggregate contributions over any intersection of identities to make claims about groups of students (e.g., Black women, disabled Latine students). We can also aggregate to make claims about the classroom overall. Because every classroom context is unique and has its own equity issues, the EQUIP methodology is customizable along modalities of participation, the qualities of an interaction (what we call *discourse dimensions*), and student social markers. Through extensive research we have found that certain customizations tend to be more useful than others, so I share practical guidance for the reader based on experience.

Modality of participation

Most of our work, including the cases in this book, has focused on verbal contributions in whole-class discussions. Verbal utterances in classroom discussions are very public and thus tightly interconnected with student status and identity.[7] Whole-class discussions can reliably be captured using a single camera or through real-time observations, which is efficient for professional development.[8] Nevertheless, our empirical work has included a wide variety of possible modalities, including small-group interactions, parallel streams of voice and chat in synchronous online settings, and even synchronous digital-teaching simulations.[9] Given the hegemony of verbal talk in classrooms, other work has focused on students' embodied engagement, including gestures, manipulatives, and visuals.[10] Such work allows us to capture contributions from students using sign language, assistive communication devices, or other modalities. The EQUIP methodology can be customized to meet a variety of research-oriented and practical goals.

Discourse dimensions

Student contributions are coded according to discourse dimensions, which capture aspects of a student's contribution and the associated teacher moves. Across studies, we have worked extensively with a half a dozen discourse dimensions (e.g., type of student talk, length of student talk, type of teacher questions, method of soliciting participation). We have also used another dozen dimensions idiosyncratically, according to individual instructor goals. Empirically, the most useful dimensions include *student talk type*, *teacher solicitation method*, and *teacher solicitation type*.[11] These dimensions are reliable across raters and explain classroom inequities. They are also actionable for instructors and thus practically useful. In the appendix on methods, I provide elaborated definitions of common dimensions and how to code them.

Briefly, both student talk type and teacher solicitation type are coded on a *Why-How-What* and *Other* continuum. *Why* talk is the deepest level, focused on explanations and justification. *How* talk focuses on processes. *What* talk focuses on answers or recall. *Other* is a catch-all category for any talk not of these three types. To increase the depth of student thinking in their classroom, instructors can move away from *What*-level talk toward *How* and *Why* talk.

Social markers

Alongside discourse dimensions, student social markers are used to generate group-level analytics. Race and gender are two social markers that apply across settings. Race and gender regularly stratify classroom participation because (1) they are visually salient aspects of our identity and (2) they are connected to broader societal stereotypes. Our research has included a wide range of other dimensions, like disability, language, socioeconomic status, and religion. Essentially, any categorical variable (i.e., multiple-choice question) can be used as a social marker. This broad conception allows us to capture status hierarchies across contexts.

Data collection and coding

The EQUIP methodology can be used in many ways, including the following:

1. An instructor records their teaching on video (with permission from their students), uploads it to share with the research team, and the research team codes it later. (This was the approach that was used in this book.)
2. A coach who is familiar with a classroom codes interactions in real-time during a regular classroom visit.
3. An instructor records and codes their own teaching, deeply reflecting on their own practice.

Each approach has trade-offs. For example, recording video supports accurate coding and allows for remote coaching but requires more technology to set up. Real-time coding allows for a coach to debrief with the instructor immediately after the lesson but may miss some interactions. Self-coding allows for greater depth of processing, due to the time spent watching video, but also requires more instructor time. Who codes the data depends on the specific goals of a program and funding available.

Equity metrics

Once a segment of classroom practice is coded, one can generate analytics about student contributions. Developing practical equity metrics about social-marker groups is nontrivial because it requires relating the participation of a group relative to the size of that group. Consider a hypothetical classroom in which there were three contributions from men and twelve from women.

These data mean little without knowing the classroom demographics. If there were an equal number of men and women in the class, perhaps alongside some nonbinary students too, the class would appear to be dominated by women. Yet, what if there was only one man and twenty-four women? This would mean that the single man spoke much more than one would predict based on demographic representation.

To coordinate participation and group size, we generate an analytic called *average contributions*, calculated as the total number of contributions from a group divided by the size of that group. In the above example, women would have 0.5 average contributions (12/24), whereas the man would have 3 average contributions (3/1). We interpret this metric as the man participating six times as much as the average woman in the class. A clear inequity. Average contributions are straightforward to interpret, and they facilitate comparisons across studies because we can compare rates of participation irrespective of the demographics of the class.[12]

The EQUIP app

To facilitate the use of the EQUIP methodology, we built a free web app (www.equip.ninja). The app allows a user to set up a virtual classroom, code student participation, and generate data analytics. Customization is built directly into the app, so it can be used for a variety of applications. This app was used to support the professional learning described in this book.

OTHER PRACTICAL MEASURES

Although the EQUIP methodology is highly customizable and thus applicable to many settings, it has limitations. For example, if instructors were interested in subjective student experiences, then developing a survey and disaggregating the results by social-marker categories could be more useful. Or if instructors wanted to know more about how students understood scientific concepts, they would be better served by a concept inventory. In general, a practical measure should:

1. be easy to deploy,
2. disaggregate by student social markers, and
3. generate actionable data that leads to changes in teaching practice.

Together, these features allow instructors to intentionally use data to support participatory equity goals. Summative assessments or course failure rates are not practical measures because they provide information that is not actionable (e.g., after a student has already failed the class). WestEd offers a repository of practical of measures that could also be used to support an equity learning community (https://mpm.wested.org). Another useful platform is Student Electronic Exit Tickets (SEET). The SEET is customizable and allows instructors to gather data from students disaggregated by student social markers (www.scienceseet.com).[13] In this book, I used the EQUIP methodology, but much of what I describe would apply to other measures too. Later in this chapter, I provide specific guidance around collecting and using data.

OVERVIEW OF EQUITY LEARNING COMMUNITIES

Broadly speaking, an equity learning community is a group of people collaborating to study issues of inequity in their own teaching practice. The community is data driven and meets regularly to process empirical data from their own classrooms, discuss issues with each other, and create action plans. Equity metrics are customized to the needs of each individual instructor. Learning communities support the relationship building needed to sustain engagement and foster concrete changes. Instructors learn from processing their own data, observing other instructors process their data, and receiving group feedback. The overarching goal of the community is for all members to become more effective and equitable teachers.

Community members make iterative, incremental changes to their practice, which they can track using data. As instructors see progress reflected in their data, it further increases their motivation and capacity for change. Immediately overhauling one's practice is not the goal. When instructors radically overhaul their practice and it doesn't go as planned, they often revert to pure lecture. In contrast, by focusing on smaller, incremental changes, instructors can experience success, as they have a measurable impact on their students, evidenced by data. Typically, an instructor will try to change *one to two things* about their practice in response to data received during a debrief meeting. When such changes are ongoing and sustained over time, they accumulate into larger shifts in practice and thinking. For this reason, based on our experiences, at least one semester, but ideally more, is needed to see large changes in practice.

FORMING AN EQUITY LEARNING COMMUNITY

Equity learning communities can take on a variety of arrangements. In general, there is a coaching team and one or more instructors. The responsibilities of the coaching team are to help collect and analyze data, provide feedback to instructors, and facilitate debrief meetings. In this book, the coaching team consisted of a lead faculty coach and graduate student coders.[14] The faculty coach was responsible for setting the stage for the learning community, facilitating, and providing support to their participants. The student coders ensured data was collected and coded and feedback was provided in a timely fashion. They also had deep inside knowledge of participants' teaching by watching their classroom videos and shared that information during debriefs. Depending on time and resources, a single coach could collect data *and* lead debrief sessions. However, we find a larger coaching team is beneficial, as it can lead to a greater diversity of perspectives. In selecting a coach, it is helpful to choose someone who has some prior experiences with teaching and facilitation (e.g., a faculty developer, an instructional technology designer, or an instructor with training in education).

After an instructor has participated for a few semesters, they may be later recruited to serve as a coach for a new learning community. These coaches can then be organized into their own learning community (a so-called coaching community) to enhance their coaching practice. Cases in this book include three participants—Brian, Kelly, and Sam—who were later recruited into a coaching community that met monthly to discuss how their coaching was going and to develop strategies and provide mutual support. I had ongoing relationships with each of the coaches because I had previously coached them when they were participants. I led the coaching community to support the next cohort of coaches. My goal was to provide guidance on coaching as well as concrete strategies that they could share with their participants. In what follows, I outline the general process and provide details for each step of facilitating an equity learning community (see figure 1.1).

INTAKE INTERVIEWS

To begin, the coaching team conducts individual intake interviews with participants.[15] These interviews help build relationships with participants in a one-on-one setting. Trust and vulnerability are a foundation for difficult conversations,

FIGURE 1.1 Flowchart for the process of forming an equity learning community

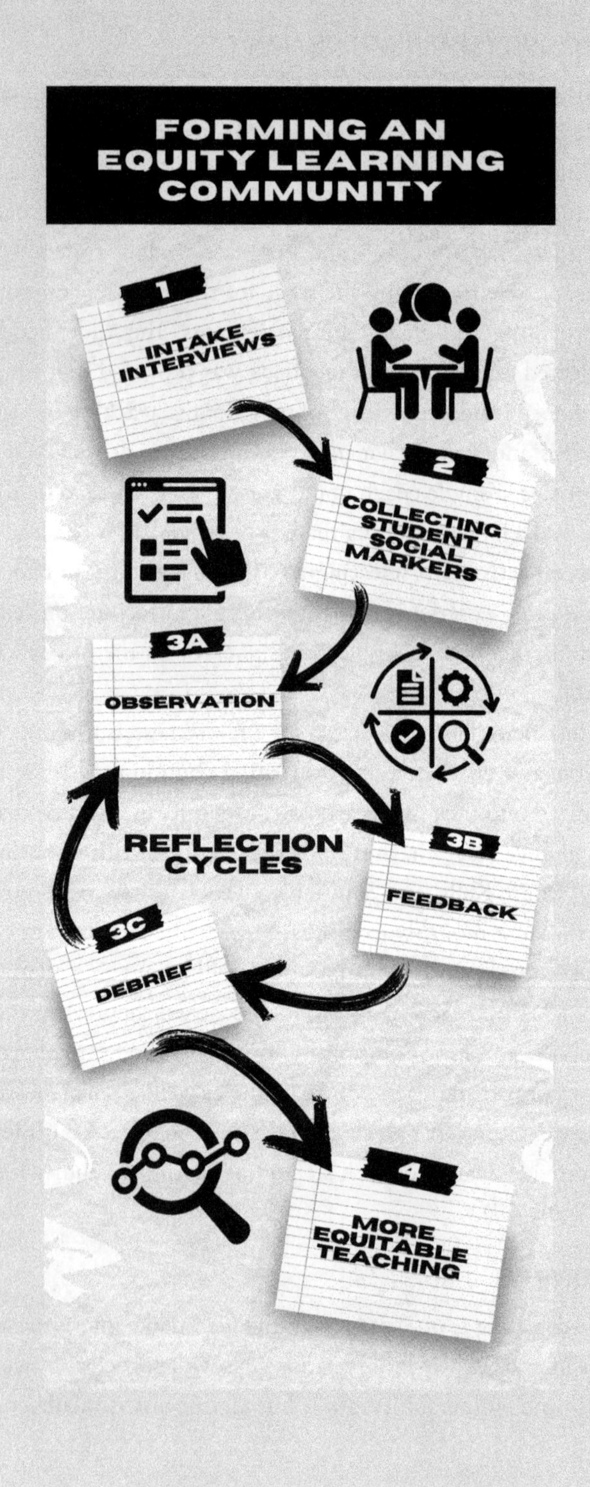

which are likely to arise in reflecting on one's own inequitable practices. The interviews serve as a vehicle to build this trust.

Second, the interviews are a learning process for participants. The interviews support instructors to externalize their understanding of classroom hierarchies—such as whether they notice and name racialized phenomena or if they have concrete teaching strategies to address them—which provides the groundwork for revision of practice. Third, the interviews provide insight into each instructor's context, enabling coaches to customize the learning process for every faculty member. In my work, I conducted intake interviews over Zoom so that they could be recorded and studied later. The interviews focused on these five main areas:[16]

1. **General background.** Focused on the instructor's discipline/research and teaching generally (these were icebreaker questions to build rapport).
2. **Equity in general.** Including how they define equity, how they conceptualize equitable teaching, how they've responded to inequities in the past, and their current equity goals.
3. **Gender equity.** Focused on discussing the instructor's identity, the role of gender on students in the discipline, and stereotypes, as well as on examining times when something related to gender came up during a class session, how they teach for equity around gender, and how their perceptions have changed over time.
4. **Racial equity.** The same set of questions as number three, except focused on race. Talking about gender is typically easier for instructors, which is why it comes first.
5. **Customizing analytics.** Choosing social markers and discourse dimensions that were relevant to the instructor's context.

In addition to gathering information about the participants, the intake interviews were used to signal a few important messages to the participants:

1. **Positionality:** I am open about my own positionality and how it impacts my work, modeling for participants what it means to recognize and be transparent about how one's positionality shapes one's perceptions.
2. **Partnership:** Participants are not mere recipients of coaching but are seen as active partners who contribute to our collective learning.

3. **Nonjudgment:** All participants come to the process at different places; my goal is to uncover what participants are thinking and use that information to guide their learning experience, not to lead them to the "correct" answer.

Taken together, these messages set the stage for the types of relationships that will be fostered in the learning community.

COLLECTING STUDENT SOCIAL MARKERS

Once the intake interview is completed, the next step is to create a student roster with social-marker data. If social-marker data are readily available (e.g., from an institutional-research department), no further data collection is needed.[17] Because these data may not be readily available, or may not include all relevant social markers, an instructor typically administers a demographic survey to their students. To maximize response rates, these surveys are administered during class time rather than after class. In my experience, when an instructor adequately describes the purpose of this work, they receive a very high response rate from students (more than 90 percent) because students want their instructors to learn how to teach better.

For students who do not respond to the survey, a backup option is for the instructor to fill in missing data where possible (e.g., the instructor might assign gender categories based on their perception of physical expression). Ambiguous social-marker expressions are coded as *unknown*. To be clear, these data may not reflect how students self-identify, but they are likely to mirror whatever implicit biases the instructor has. This makes instructor-provided data an imperfect but potentially useful tool for reflection.

Reflection cycles

An equity learning community is organized around reflection cycles. Ideally, the community meets monthly (four cycles per semester) to promote ongoing engagement through enough cycles to enact change. Having fewer cycles limits instructional change, and spreading out the time between cycles results in lost momentum. Practically, meetings begin about five weeks into the semester, which provides time for an intake interview, for class rosters to stabilize, and for demographics to be collected. Consequently, the four "monthly" meetings happen roughly every three weeks. Each cycle has three main components: (1) observation, (2) feedback, and (3) debrief. Below, I outline each of these steps in more depth.

The first few meetings are oriented toward building trust and community. Depending on where participants enter the conversation, they may not be prepared to tackle thorny issues like racial inequity from the offset. In such cases, starting with more general conversations about productive discourse—later leading into gender equity and then, finally, racial equity—can provide an easier onramp for instructors who have not previously been involved in this work. Other instructors will dive deep from the outset. With the EQUIP methodology, social-marker data are always present, and thus, identity-based inequities can be weaved seamlessly into conversations.

Observation. Observations provide the raw data for generating equity metrics. The type of observation—whether video recorded or in real-time—can be chosen to fit the needs of the community. Instructors typically share photo rosters (video screenshots annotated with student names) to help the coding team identify students. Once the observation is performed, the coaching team codes the data to generate equity metrics. While video is imperfect, our experience is that most contributions can be coded (more than 90 percent).[18] Identifying students is further supported by good teaching practices such as using student names and name tents. Coding accuracy also improves over time as coders are familiarized with the classroom.

Feedback. Once data are coded, each instructor receives a descriptive feedback report. These reports provide a nonjudgmental summary of classroom participation. We identify salient trends with respect to prior reports, making growth visible. These summaries consist of numerical values and relevant graphs, typically taken from the EQUIP app. We also provide our qualitative impressions, highlighting strengths and potential areas for improvement. These impressions often center on specific classroom episodes, which can be used as fodder for conversation during the debrief. If available, short video clips of these relevant events are an effective way to ground the conversation. Finally, we include a few concrete teaching strategies to redress observed inequities. For example, we might suggest a five-hands strategy (waiting for five students to raise their hand before calling on someone) to attenuate participation from a single dominant student and elicit a broader range of contributions from others.

Feedback reports are provided to instructors before the debrief meetings to provide processing time. Classroom observations, especially concerning equity, put instructors in a very vulnerable state. Because data describe inequities, instructors may experience frustration or even shame in response to the data they receive. Processing time combined with a supportive community conversation helps put instructors in the right frame of mind to productively improve. Beyond suggesting instructional strategies, it is the job of the coaching community to help instructors process these potentially difficult feelings. By building trust and in-it-togetherness within the community, coaches can help instructors see the inequities as tied to larger systems of oppression, not as their own individual shortcomings, and build motivation to teach better. For some examples in this book, Gwen changed her conceptions of equity, and Elayne learned to build a more culturally responsive curriculum.

Debrief. After processing feedback reports, instructors join a community debrief.[19] This important event requires the coaching team to be fully present to support instructors. How these meetings are managed can make or break whether instructors will improve their instruction. Feedback reports open the conversation but require unpacking from the community to result in meaningful action. Coaches help manage the feelings of all participants, provide a broader context to understanding inequities, give concrete suggestions to instructors, and build community to empower instructors to support each other. This is not a simple task.

The community element of debrief meetings allows instructors to see how others process through the data they receive. This highlights the ubiquity of inequities across contexts. Moreover, when a participant models humility and openness in response to data rather than defensiveness, it opens space for others in the community to do the same. To support such collective learning, it is helpful to create learning communities in which at least one or two members are likely to be very open from the outset. If all instructors are defensive and closed, this can reverberate across instructors and shut down conversations.

Instructors are often isolated on their campuses and may lack opportunities to talk with others about teaching (especially since the COVID-19 pandemic). Academics tend to be overworked and are more likely to gravitate toward activities that they find rewarding and useful. This builds community in highly competitive and often individualized fields. For instance, one of the participants in this study, Gwen, highlighted the comfort she felt knowing that any time something happened in her classroom, she could look forward to a community event to process through it with like-minded peers.

GUIDANCE ON DATA COLLECTION

Here, I provide practical guidance on selecting social markers and discourse dimensions, generating a student roster, and identifying students.

Student social markers

Each instructor chooses which social markers they will track. The choice of social markers should be grounded in the hierarchies that are present in a specific context, discipline, or region.[20] Choosing two to four social markers per classroom tends to work well. This requires an instructor to test their hypothesis of what drives power dynamics in their classroom rather than simply choosing all available social markers, which is unfocused and thus less effective.[21] Given their visible salience, we typically include race and gender.[22] Additional social markers can lead to other insights. For example, considering disability or language proficiency alongside race allows for more nuanced intersectional analyses.

Operationalizing social markers. Social markers are social constructions. There are no natural categorizations for race and ethnicity, gender, disability, or other social identities. How these constructs are taken up has shifted throughout history and depends on local context. Consequently, the coaching team and instructors must work together productively to operationalize social markers. Consider the racial categories of *Asian* or *Asian American*. For example, while those categories might be useful in a context where there are few Asian American students, they obscure remarkable diversity in Asian populations. Accordingly, for classrooms with many Asian students, creating multiple categories for multiple populations of Asian heritage is probably more effective. Similarly, questions of racial and ethnic identity for Latine populations are complicated. While it may make sense to incorporate Latine populations together in some cases, in other situations it may not. Across racial and ethnic groups, there are a wide variety of complexities to consider; for example, should Black American and Black African students be considered in the same group?

Mixed-race students add another level of nuance. As a result of globalization, classrooms are increasingly filled with students of mixed racial heritages. A catch-all mixed-race category is accurate but limited. A White Asian student has different racialized experiences than an Afro-Latino student. How to identify students is a complex process based on student identification, public presentation, and local power dynamics. In general, we lead the process based on students' personal identification. When this results in many categories (more than five or six), we typically condense categories based on how different students might be *perceived* socially. This is an imperfect process and could sometime be fraught with false assumptions.

Maximizing social-marker categories for greater fidelity may have less practical utility, obscuring common experiences across minoritized populations. Moreover, when groups are so small (only one to two students in each), group-level analytics lose their meaning. Generally, we aim to have between three to six values for any social-marker category; for example, for race and ethnicity, we might use *Asian*, *Black*, *Latine*, *Native*, *White*, and *Other*. In some studies, we have allowed for two variables, *Race 1* and *Race 2*, where one of the variables has more values (thus higher accuracy) and the other is more condensed. Ultimately, there is no absolute truth in how social markers are defined; this is a sensemaking process at the discretion of instructors and coaches in service of practical equity.

Other social markers also present issues for operationalization. Consider socioeconomic status. How do you measure it? Asking students about their income (or parental income) might feel intrusive. Alternatively, as we have done, one could ask questions such as "How many hours do you work in a week?" or "Do you work?" with possible responses being "full-time," "part-time," or "no." Another way to operationalize socioeconomic status is to ask about financial aid. In a K–12 setting, information about whether a student receives a free or reduced-price lunch classification may be readily available to teachers.

Consider disability. Simply asking the question "Do you have a disability?" is ambiguous. A clearer approach would be to offer choices:

- "Yes, with a formal diagnosis."
- "Yes, without a formal diagnosis."
- "No."
- "Do not wish to disclose."

An alternative would be to ask, "Do you identify as disabled?" and provide appropriate response options. This would focus more on identity and less on medical classification. Another option is to ask, "Do you receive classroom accommodations?"

- "Yes."
- "No, but I am eligible."
- "No."

In an inclusive classroom space with a greater focus on disability, one could craft questions with more specificity around types of disabilities or simply allow students to write in their own responses. In a K–12 setting, whether students have an Individualized Education Plan (IEP) or a 504 Accommodations Plan could be used as social markers. In summary, operationalizing social markers is a complex sensemaking process, requiring intentionality.

Student roster

Social-marker data are compiled into a student roster. A typical roster consists of a spreadsheet with students as rows and social markers as columns. A spreadsheet formatted this way can be pasted directly into the EQUIP app.

Selecting discourse dimensions

We typically use three to five discourse dimensions when we are coding videos. I would recommend even fewer for real-time coding, to keep up with the fast pace of classroom practice. Often, less is more. Adding more dimensions increases coding time, and discourse dimensions tend to be correlated. Within each dimension, we use two to four levels (with a possible additional level of *N/A*). Again, less is more, as additional levels complexify the coding process and obscure patterns because the data are too finely sorted. A practical approach is to start with three dimensions—student talk type, teacher solicitation method, and teacher solicitation type—and customize one to two additional dimensions that instructors wish for. These three dimensions are described in the appendix on methods.

Identifying students

Social-marker specificity requires attaching contributions to specific students. We typically use a photo roster and encourage instructors to use student names or have student name tents. Here, I provide deeper guidance to ensure coding accuracy.

Field notes. When an observer attends a class session, it allows them to generate a content log and field notes during the observation. This allows the observer to identify (with time stamps) all student speakers. This can be used for real-time coding or in conjunction with a video. Chunking the observation into different segments (e.g., launch, small groups, whole-class discussion) further supports efficient coding. An observer can record events of interest, either to debrief in real-time or to later include in a feedback report.

Triangulating identification. Some student contributions may be unidentifiable on a video recording. We still record such contributions (labeling them as "Unknown Student") because often the same student participates later and can be identified, allowing the initial contribution to be completed. If the speaker remains unidentifiable, a screenshot can be sent to the instructor to see if they can identify the student.

Partial transcripts. The EQUIP app does not require transcripts for coding. Nonetheless, we often generate partial transcripts to support coding. These transcripts record student speech with time stamps and only small amounts of relevant instructor speech. Generating a record in addition to coding in the EQUIP app supports discussion or further research on specific episodes.

Student privacy. Student privacy is also an important concern. Education research requires approval from an Institutional Review Board. Professional learning doesn't typically require such formal approval, but it is still important to protect student privacy in accordance with a schools' policies and ethical best practices. This means providing clear opportunities for students to opt out and making all best efforts not to capture those students on video (e.g., by seating them on one side of the room away from the camera). Video must be handled with care and not shared with others unless appropriate permissions are obtained.

GUIDANCE FOR COACHES

The effectiveness of the coaching team will have a profound impact on the results of an equity learning community. Former participants can be effective coaches. Having emotionally experienced participants processing their own data enhances empathy and relationship building. Further, they have had coaching skills modeled for them. Familiarity with education research, teaching experience, and prior experiences within leadership and facilitation roles will all support coaches to empower their instructors. There are a variety of resources on coaching, including one I coauthored from a previous project.[23] I have also written a book on equitable teaching strategies in higher education, which is filled with practical strategies I have used with former participants in equity learning communities.[24]

Coach and instructor positionality

Aim for diversity across multiple dimensions of identity in the coaching team. It is often easier for people to trust others who they see as more "like them," and conversely, more difficult to trust those who seem more different. Personally, as a White disabled person, I can more easily connect with other disabled people. Also, living in a racist society, I recognize that many instructors of color have had negative prior experiences with White people doing equity work. Accordingly, I try to approach the work with humility, aiming to build personal relationships and trust. Further, when there is diversity across the coaching team and instructors, it provides opportunities for mutual understanding, if approached with a learner's mindset.

Recruitment and outreach

Effective recruitment bolsters the success of an equity learning community. Because learning communities support both individual and collective learning, group dynamics impact everyone's success. To support access to this learning opportunity, I advise putting out an open call for participants (e.g., on a campus mailing list or through a Center for Teaching and Learning). Simultaneously, intentional recruitment of other instructors—especially those who are likely to be responsive to the feedback they receive—helps create positive group dynamics. Snowball sampling, in which participants recruit further participants, helps create groups where some participants already know each other, allowing for more trust from the outset. The appendixes offer sample text for recruitment. This was used in campus contexts that were favorable toward equity. In less-favorable political climates, I would recommend creating a more general call focused on instructional improvement instead of equity and screening participants through intake interviews.

Structuring a debrief session

I typically structure debriefs as one-hour sessions, which balances instructor time commitments with sufficient processing time. Generally, I begin each session with a quick check-in, asking how everyone's doing, how their classes are going, and if they had any new insights or celebrations from their data. Giving each participant an opportunity to share briefly helps orient everyone to the meeting. This process typically takes ten minutes or less.

There are a variety of ways to structure the bulk of the meeting. Early in the semester, especially during the first debrief, I may intentionally focus on an instructor who I perceive as more receptive to feedback. By asking the instructor before the meeting if it is okay to dive into their data, it sets them into a more open frame of mind. Then, through productive conversations around data with that instructor, the process becomes less threatening for others.

Coaches must balance the depth and breadth of conversations. It is generally possible to do a deep dive into data for only one to two instructors in a meeting. Other instructors can still benefit from the collective processing of data and productive modeling of openness in response to feedback. In addition to deep dives, I ensure there is a brief check-in with everyone in the group. Alternatively, time can be spread more evenly across participants. Because there is less processing time, I would tend to use this approach only later, after a community is established, and instructors are better positioned to process their data more productively with less scaffolding. Each meeting I connect back to each instructor's goals and their progress implementing different strategies. One way to support this is by either selecting short video clips (shared with instructor permission) or having instructors choose their own short clips. Seeing teaching practices humanizes the equity metrics and can make conversations more concrete.

Before closing a meeting, each instructor should commit to at least one teaching practice they plan to implement during the next cycle. This is imperative. Without setting concrete action plans, instructors are more likely to talk about data but do little to change their teaching practice. By connecting practices to data, instructors can track the impact of their actions over time. If instructors are not systematic in their use of new strategies, and there isn't support or accountability to use those strategies, the whole process can derail. Shared meeting notes with action items can help instructors remember which goals they are working on. Post-meeting emails can also clarify the discussion and action items.

General principles for facilitation

The coaching team should ensure community meetings are productive. For example, an instructor might process their data and conclude that no changes are needed. This is an opportunity for a coach to intervene and support the instructor to continue to improve. Having observed hundreds of classrooms, we recognize that, for even the most experienced instructors, there is always room for growth. We frame the learning community as an opportunity for lifelong growth.

Alternatively, suppose an instructor has high levels of participation from a minoritized group and decides that they should attenuate that participation (e.g., "My Black students are talking too much and White students are left behind"). We respond to this by situating the present within historical inequities in society and in their discipline. When a coach has built a trusting environment, it helps mitigate defensiveness during a potentially difficult conversation. Here are some common pitfalls and general strategies for keeping the community on track.

Mitigating power dynamics. Ironically, even when equity conversations are designed to disrupt power dynamics, those same dynamics often manifest. For example, I have witnessed many men take up a disproportionate amount of talk time in conversations about gender equity. Similarly, White instructors may center themselves in race conversations (e.g., by talking too much, focusing on their own guilt, using White tears). Such situations require intervention to ensure that learning community meetings remain equitable. By structuring talk opportunities, rather than having a "free-for-all," it is much easier to ensure specific community members don't dominate. A general principle is to center the voices and experiences of people who are most impacted by a particular issue such as racism, sexism, or ableism.

Promoting social-marker talk. In my experience, many instructors attribute lack of student success to innate student characteristics, calling them slow, fast, lazy, privileged, strong, weak, shy, and so forth. These deficit-oriented attributions shift the focus to what students lack rather than what an instructor can do to better support their students. To counter this, coaches can bring the conversation back to social markers. For example, if an instructor attributes the lack of participation from a woman in their class to "shyness," the facilitator could connect this back to gender socialization, masculine disciplinary norms, and the consistency of male-dominated patterns across contexts.[25] Equity metrics facilitate this process through social-marker specificity. I find that asking questions about what students *can do* rather than what they *cannot do* can also help shift conversations away from deficits to strengths. As a facilitator, building on the strengths of instructors who utilize social-marker talk is also an effective way of modeling it for other instructors who are more reticent.

Distinguishing intent and impact. I assume instructors who volunteer for a learning community are well intentioned. These good intentions are often associated with our visions of ourselves as "good people." Simultaneously, good intentions can have negative consequences. Although an instructor may have students simply shout out answers rather than raising hands because their goal is to create a "comfortable environment," the actual impact could be to create a White-male-dominated space. Similarly, some microaggressions may result from curiosity. Consider the well-meaning professor who comments on the Black student's writing that "it is very articulate." Or says to the Latino student, "Your English is really good!" These supposed compliments may be experienced as harmful.[26] The coaching team can help instructors untangle differences in intent and impact across settings.

Managing levels of awareness. Instructors in an equity learning community will vary in their lived experiences and their teaching experiences. Consequently, a coach must manage varying levels of awareness of inequities. For example, White participants have fewer lived experiences of racialization and thus typically have less understanding of racism. Other participants will have direct experiences with ableism, sexism, or other forms of oppression. It is important not to equate these oppressions (e.g., a White woman who compares sexism to racism), or to play oppression Olympics (comparing who has it worse). A guiding principle is to center the lived experiences and knowledge of individuals who are most impacted by any system of oppression. Individuals should take extra care when addressing issues of oppression that they do not personally experience. Especially when difficult conversations arise, such as around race, I would prioritize the perspectives of people of color compared to White colleagues who may feel bad for having committed microaggressions against others. Overall, a learning community should be oriented toward learning and should be a safe place to make mistakes, but when levels of awareness are highly mismatched, it may be better to place certain individuals into different learning communities.

WHO SHOULD JOIN AN EQUITY LEARNING COMMUNITY?

Anyone can benefit from an equity learning community, but some will likely benefit more than others. While this book highlights cases of instructors who were largely successful as participants, some instructors we have worked with benefited less from the process. Analyzing the characteristics of different participants and their outcomes has led to some general guidance for selecting participants, provided here.

To begin, participation should always be voluntary, never forced. Mandating someone to participate in such an equity initiative has a high likelihood of backlash or at least disengagement from participants. My experience is that instructors who have some experience with active learning (e.g., facilitating classroom conversations beyond pure lecture) and some awareness of inequities are likely to benefit from an equity learning community. Individuals who want to teach more equitably but lack concrete strategies to do so make ideal participants. This desire to improve tends to lead to more openness and less defensiveness.

Who is less likely to benefit? Instructors who use pure lecture or who have never facilitated a discussion are still learning the basic mechanics of teaching and thus lack the skills to enact equitable teaching. Similarly, instructors who aren't convinced active student engagement is important are likely to revert to pure lecture when they encounter difficulties using new strategies. We have worked with instructors in both categories who made only modest changes to their teaching after a semester of engaging in an equity learning community. Alternatively, instructors with decades of experience lecturing might perceive themselves as experts and be less open to change. Another barrier is formal evaluations. Instructors without secure employment may be driven by external evaluations that require traditional teaching and thus be less able to change. Intake interviews are a mechanism to screen for participants who are most likely to succeed or to create multiple learning communities while managing different levels of awareness.

The current study

This book is organized around six instructors who participated in equity learning communities (see table 1.1). These longitudinal cases allow the reader to see the learning process of the instructors unfold over time. All participants had some experience with active learning. These instructors were supported by a total of four different student researchers. Rather than focusing on my own coaching approach, I highlight productive aspects of coaching from former participants to demonstrate the potential scalability of this model.

TABLE 1.1 Equity learning community participants

Name	*Institution type*	*Discipline*	*Race*	*Gender*	*Social-marker focus*	*Semesters of participation*	*Semesters of coaching*
Anne	Elite, private liberal arts	Mathematics	White	Woman	Gender	2	—
Brian	Public, Hispanic-serving	Mathematics	Black	Man	Race	1	2
Elayne	Public, Hispanic-serving	Public health	White	Woman	Race	2	—
Gwen	Private	Mathematics	Asian	Woman	Gender & Race	2	—
Kelly	Public, Hispanic-serving	Counseling	Biracial (Black/ White)	Woman	Race	2	2
Sam	Public, Hispanic-Serving	Engineering	White	Man	Gender & Race	3	2

Participants varied in disciplinary backgrounds and racial and gender identities. Overall, instructors were committed to equity, each with a set of relevant life experiences that helped them grasp some of the nuances of inequity in education. Some participants could articulate specific teaching practices for equity, while others could not. Overall, participants did not have specific practices that they would draw upon to disrupt gender, racial, socioeconomic, or other inequities in their classes. In other words, the instructors had relevant background and interest, but they were by no means experts in equitable teaching before they joined a learning community.

The six case studies highlight different aspects of an equity learning community. For Anne and Gwen, I detail each of their learning cycles to unpack the process in depth. These participants each have their own chapter. Both Anne and Gwen were coached by former participants (Brian and Kelly, respectively). The next chapter highlights Elayne and Sam, providing a longitudinal summary over multiple semesters. The chapter after that describes Brian and Kelly, with brief reflections from their participant experiences and an emphasis on their coaching practices. Detailed information about the study, participants, design, and protocols can be found in the appendix on methodology.

In the case studies that follow, I highlight a few key takeaways for facilitating equity learning communities. Although these takeaways come up across the chapters, I highlight specific ones within certain chapters that serve as exemplars. Here I summarize the takeaways to prime the reader to look out for them when reading the chapters that follow.

Anne's case

- *Data provide motivation and capacity for change.* In Anne's case, data initially showed stark gender inequities in classroom participation. This brought urgency to her goal to improve gender equity in her classroom. Later in the semester, when data began to show evidence of gender-equity improvements, this allowed her to see exactly how new strategies were producing more equitable student engagement.
- *Incremental changes accumulate to a larger impact.* Anne adopted a few very effective strategies that had a direct impact on gendered participation in her classroom. Nonetheless, core elements of Anne's teaching remained the same. She did not need to change everything—she just needed to make certain adjustments to enhance equity.

Gwen's case

- *Equitable teaching supports specific students.* As a mathematics educator, from the outset, Gwen was already using many teaching practices as suggested by the research literature. The biggest shift that Gwen needed to make was using these strategies with more intentionality. To disrupt classroom inequities, instructors can provide targeted support to specific students (often based on social-marker identities) to elevate their status and engagement.
- *Instructor perspectives and practices can shift together.* Alongside changing her teaching practices, during her first semester of participation, Gwen's notion of what constituted equity shifted as well. She grappled with various ways to conceptualize equity, eventually working to intentionally redress historical inequities as a key feature of improving equity.

Elayne's and Sam's cases

- *Instructors develop responsibility for their students.* Both Elayne and Sam reflected on how their perspectives about student participation shifted.

Initially, Elayne and Sam viewed participating or not as primarily a student responsibility. Later, after data revealed how specific teaching moves could broaden classroom participation, Elayne and Sam came to appreciate the power an instructor has to shape engagement in their classroom.

- *Change continues beyond participation in the equity learning community.* Elayne and Sam's cases detail multiple semesters of learning within equity learning communities. However, even after this coaching, instructors often continue to improve upon the foundation built during their engagement. Especially in Elayne's case, after her coaching was completed, she continued to experiment and develop a more culturally responsive curriculum.

Brian's and Kelly's cases

- *Relationships provide the foundation for change.* Equity work is vulnerable and requires trust. As coaches, Brian and Kelly intentionally fostered their relationships with their instructors in ways that supported them to have difficult conversations about equity and inequity. This relationship building provided the foundation for concrete changes to instructional practice.
- *Experiences as a participant support coaching.* Brian and Kelly leveraged their prior experiences as equity learning community participants to serve as effective coaches. These prior experiences gave them a model of what coaching could look like, and crucially, it allowed them to relate to their participants because they could share their own experiences of processing data and changing their teaching in response to that data. This gave credibility to Brian and Kelly serving in the coaching role.

Overall, these eight takeaways directly connect back to the three core features of an equity learning community: (1) Empirical data create local urgency; (2) learning communities collaboratively process the data; and (3) instructors make iterative, incremental changes to practice. As coaches build trust within their communities, that trust allows instructors to use the data in ways that supports instructional change. This change also extends to instructor perspectives and can continue even after the equity learning community disbands.

CHAPTER 2

Anne's Story: Using Incremental Change to Transform Instruction

Equity learning communities use incremental change to transform instruction. This chapter focuses on Anne, whose story is an exemplar of incremental improvements to practice, as evidenced by reductions in gender inequity in her classroom. Anne is a full professor in mathematics who was teaching at an elite private university when we visited her classroom. This case highlights two key takeaways.

Data provide motivation and capacity for change. Anne's story illustrates the paradox of equitable teaching. Even as a woman who had succeeded in mathematics and who had been a strong advocate for women in mathematics for many years, her vision of gender equity did not necessarily translate into her classroom learning environment. When she received data showing these inequities quantitatively, it brought a new sense of urgency to redress them. Later in the semester, when she received data showing she was making progress in reducing inequities, it sustained her motivation and capacity for change.

Incremental changes accumulate to a larger impact. Anne's case highlights the power of small ongoing, incremental changes. Over the course of her participation, the core of Anne's pedagogy remained similar, but with the support of data and the learning community, she became more intentional in her approach and learned to use a few high-leverage teaching practices. As such, her case illustrates how even a few specific changes to one's teaching practice can have a dramatic impact on students. This chapter details Anne's process of transforming her classroom from one in which women were on the sidelines to one where women were often leading discussions. Even more impressive, this happened in a mathematics classroom, which has a long-standing history of gender inequity.

This case illustrates the role of the equity learning community in helping Anne process her data and in sharing concrete action items in response to the observed inequities. By the end of the semester, Anne had dramatically increased participation from women and had transformed the *types* of participation in her classroom, with students explaining and justifying their ideas, rather than simply providing answers (concrete data are provided in figures 2.1 and 2.2 later in the chapter). Finally, this case demonstrates how, despite our best intentions, some practices may not enact our beliefs, and it is therefore beneficial to have data and thought partners to inform and help us transform our practices. In this chapter, I provide a brief overview of Anne's background, work through her four reflection cycles in the learning community, and close with her reflections on the process.

ANNE'S PROFILE

Anne is a White woman who had been teaching mathematics for thirty years at the time of the study, most recently at an elite private university. She is an applied mathematician who also has a strong professional interest in helping women advance in the discipline. For example, she has served within high-profile professional roles in the discipline that helped mentor women. As an instructor, she aims to help students see the value of mathematics through applications. One way she enacts that is by allowing students to work on problems with real-world importance. Anne was teaching in a face-to-face classroom during her time in the learning community.

Anne participated in an equity learning community for two semesters, with one other faculty participant, Ramesh, coach Brian (described in a later chapter), and student coder Marie. Here, I focus on the first semester of participation to illustrate Anne's learning process in-depth and show what is possible within just four debrief meetings over a semester.

During her first semester of participation, Anne was teaching linear algebra. For many students, linear algebra is one of the first mathematics classes that they encounter that is focused primarily on abstract mathematics, including logic, argumentation, and proof. This contrasts with earlier courses, like calculus and differential equations, that are often more about computations and

TABLE 2.1 Demographics in Anne's class (fall 2021, in person)

		Race/Ethnicity		
		Asian	White	**Total**
Gender	Man	7	11	18
	Woman	6	5	11
	Total	13	16	29

solving problems. The demographics of Anne's class are shown in table 2.1. Given that the racial demographics were relatively homogeneous, and given her own professional aspirations, Anne focused primarily on gender equity in her intervention work.

In her intake interview, Anne described equity as a situation in which "everyone gets to pursue their own dreams." Anne focused mostly on gender equity, as it was salient for her as a woman in mathematics who grew up regularly being told "girls can't do X." Anne grew up without many role models of women in mathematics and saw herself as someone who had to carve her own path despite these circumstances. Although she loved mathematics, she also felt that some people in the field could be toxic and sometimes sexist. Beyond gender barriers, Anne remarked how students of color—and especially women of color—faced additional barriers and had to contend with more microaggressions. Overall, Anne situated inequities as structural and institutional problems that needed to be addressed, not as student deficits.

Before participating in the learning community, Anne described her approach to equitable teaching as "removing barriers" that students in her discipline face. One way she did this was "removing the judgment" from mathematics so students could "build their self-confidence." Practically, this meant that Anne didn't use timed tests. She also allowed for corrections on assignments to emphasize growth over performance and teach her students that making mistakes is a part of learning. She also used free resources, when possible, to reduce financial barriers for some students. Despite her best intentions, Anne couldn't articulate specific strategies to promote racial or gender equity. She did mention that she had previously used random calling methods to increase participation, but she was not happy with the outcome, so she stopped using them.

REFLECTION CYCLES

Observation one

Anne's first observation took place before she met with her coach and learning community. This provided a baseline of her teaching style, which was best described as an interactive lecture. The class session was mostly led by the instructor, but throughout the session she asked questions to the students, checked for understanding, and made genuine attempts to help the students feel comfortable and engaged (e.g., through using real-world examples).

In the observed lesson, Anne introduced the concept of matrix multiplication through real-world examples such as grocery shopping and manufacturing computers. These examples were designed to help students connect the abstract mathematics of linear algebra to their everyday lived experiences, as shown in the following episode of classroom practice.

ANNE: Back at the factory, remember that each of these components for the computers require a certain amount of base elements: copper, zinc, glass, plastic, et cetera. So, if I ask the question, I want to make ten T1s, twenty-one T2s, and eleven T3s, how much of the *raw* materials of copper, zinc, glass, and plastic, will I need? Any thoughts?

[*Anne pauses for a couple of seconds; students are silent.*]

ANNE: What if I said, How much copper is needed to make all the stuff for the T1s? How much copper? [*Anne pauses again, but students are still silent.*] I need two units of copper for each transistor, two units for each resistor, and three for each computer chip. For the T1s, I need five transistors, seven resistors, and twenty buttons.

RAJ: [*Raises hand*] thirty-six.

ANNE: How did you get thirty-six?

RAJ: Um, two times five in the first row, two times seven, and three times four.

ANNE: Right, so I need two units of copper for each transistor, and I need five transistors. That gives me two times five, ten units of copper for just the transistors. So, another way to say that, is that you take the dot product of the first row and the first column, and that will give me the amount of copper just for the T1s.

In this example, Anne presented the material while asking clarifying questions to her students. Twice Anne pauses after asking a question, but there was no student response. Each unanswered question was simplified and asked again until her open-ended question had been reduced to a simple computation. Although Anne earnestly tried to engage her students in deeper thinking, she did not yet have the needed facilitation strategies.

Anne continued to describe the dot products related to computer manufacturing, and then asked her students what size of matrix their multiplication would produce. After a few different student guesses, she focused the students on the possible answer of four-*by*-three.

ANNE: So how many people think we'll end up with a four-*by*-three? [*Students raise hands.*] How many people don't know what I'm talking about? [*Edward raises his hand.*] Okay, thank you, Edward. Very brave. [*Ariel shakes her hand side by side.*] And Ariel is so-so. Thank you for being open.

ANNE: So, we're going to end up with a four-*by*-three.

In this episode, Anne's students (Edward and Ariel) felt comfortable expressing their confusion. Anne validated this confusion by labeling Edward as brave. This connected to Anne's overall philosophy of helping students feel comfortable to take risks.

After this episode, Anne worked out a general case of matrix multiplication and provided a formal definition. She connected the discussion to prior work in the class, when they had proven that matrices formed a vector space. The lesson continued, and she explicitly brought Edward back into the discussion.

ANNE: For example, try to multiply out these two matrices. First do A times B, what do you get? Remember the way we do this? What's the definition? So, Edward, I'll pick on you because you're so brave. What size matrix will I get?

[*Edward Holds up two fingers on each hand to gesture two-by-two.*]

In this episode, Anne again validated Edward's risk-taking as a valued mathematical practice. She also gave him another chance to answer a question and be successful. These examples highlight Anne's general teaching style. It was instructor-led, but she showed genuine interest in her students and their understanding. She attempted to learn her students' names and validate their feelings and possible confusions.

Learning community session one

Before the first learning community debrief, Anne received her data and had time to process patterns of student participation. During the first observation, EQUIP data showed that there were 16 student contributions from 12 different students (41 percent of the class), indicating that no individual student dominated the discussion. The type of student talk was mostly at a *What* level (13 contributions), with a few examples of *How* talk (3 contributions). This indicates that students were mostly contributing by recalling facts or providing answers, but not explaining their thinking in-depth.

These contributions were split by race, with 8 from White students and 8 from Asian students. Of these contributions, 12 of them came from men, and only 4 were from women. This amounted to 0.7 average contributions for men and only 0.36 for women, meaning that men had twice as many participation opportunities on average. The gender marginalization in this classroom profile is consistent with what I've observed elsewhere across hundreds of classroom settings.

The dominance of participation from men became a focal point for the first debrief. Anne commented directly on these patterns of inequity.

> I really want to address this business of the women not speaking. It bothers me. It just doesn't go away. They have a woman standing up in front of them, and they talk to me outside of class, but it's so hard, the social structures are so entrenched.

Anne wasn't surprised by her data, but she was upset with it. Anne brought up her prior attempts to use random calling, including her dissatisfaction with the method because putting students on the spot created a stressful situation. Instead of cold-calling students, Marie offered the "five-hands" strategy of waiting for five students to raise their hand before calling on anyone. This requires students to raise their hands rather than shouting out answers, as they did in Anne's first lesson. Moreover, this includes additional wait time for students to think before responding and gives Anne more control in choosing which student to answer her question. These features of the strategy slow down classroom practice and avoid having the loudest voices—which tend to belong to men—shouting out answers as quickly as possible.

Brian further suggested that Anne could use her data to intentionally select students who were not participating and draw them into the conversation. Marie operationalized this suggestion as follows:

> When you have a student who's very active in groups but quiet in the whole-class sessions, you can go up to them and check their work in the group and say like "Hey, when we go back, would you mind sharing your answer?" So rather than calling on the whole group, you ask the individual student to share.

This strategy is built on the idea of *assigning competence* from Complex Instruction.[1] The strategy works because it allows an instructor to intentionally select a student who is perceived as lower status but has valuable ideas to contribute. By talking to the student during work time, it avoids a situation of cold calling and allows the instructor to positively highlight their disciplinary contributions in a public space. Anne was a willing participant and began using these ideas in her teaching.

The learning community also briefly touched on the type of student talk and discussed how the above two strategies could also help students to provide deeper responses than factual recall.

Observation two

Anne began her lesson with students working in pairs to solve a matrix equation. Her classroom was ideal for partner work, as students were seated at small tables with two chairs each. Although Anne did not use partner work during the baseline observation, after her first learning community debrief, she began to use it regularly to break up her lessons. While students worked on the problem, Anne circulated around the room talking with her students. Afterward, Anne brought the students together for a whole-class discussion.

ANNE: Let's reconvene because some people are having more fun than others. And that's not fair! [*Anne begins working out the solution.*]

ANNE: So, we have a system of equations. We turn the system into $Ax = b$. We turn that system into matrix form. So that's the first step. Did everyone get that? And, then, how does the inverse help you?

BRIANA [*not called on*]: If we multiply things by [the inverse], then we get the inverse on one side, which is just x.

ANNE: So, we multiply both sides by A inverse, and get $x = A$ inverse b. [working out computations]

ANNE: [*Rose raises hand.*] What did you get Rose?

ROSE: Sixteen-thirds minus four-thirds minus seven-thirds.

ANNE: Really? Let's just see. [*Works out computation.*]

Anne continued working out the problem collaboratively with the students. In this episode, students more readily volunteered their ideas because they had sufficient think time during their partner work. In contrast, during her baseline lesson, when Anne tried to develop mathematical ideas purely in the whole-class discussion, it did not provide time for students to work out their in-progress thinking. Briana, who volunteered her ideas without being called on, was someone who did not participate during the first observation. Thus, by making the simple change of incorporating student work time, Anne was able to broaden participation in her discussions.

Anne also practiced using discourse moves to solicit multiple ideas in response to her questions. For example, after students offered an idea, she asked questions like "All right, anyone else?" She also used student names to give students ownership over their ideas, making statements such as "Is it possible that Amelia got a different solution from Raj?"

Later in her lesson, Anne created another opportunity for partner work. This time, she practiced the strategy suggested by Marie. She consulted with students during work time, and when she discovered that a pair of women had the correct response, she asked them if they would be willing to share during the whole-class debrief.

ANNE: I want to know: what is the relationship between these three spaces? The row space, null space, and column space of the matrix *A* in a row-reduced form. Makes sense? [*Anne pauses.*] Talk to your partner for a moment, and ask, Are they the same? Are these two spaces the same? Are they related at all? If you have an answer, you've got to have a reason for that answer.

[*Students talk in pairs for about six minutes.*]

ANNE: Let's come together and talk about these. These aren't really easy questions, right? That's great, because otherwise you wouldn't be learning anything. All right. How about Abigail and Suparna; what did you decide about the row space?

ABIGAIL: We decided that the row spaces are equivalent because *A* and its image are both equivalent.

ANNE: So, the word *row equivalent* . . . you think these are equal? What does *B* being row equivalent to *A* mean?

ABIGAIL: It means that any linear combination of *B* also contains part of *A*, the row space of *A*.

ANNE: Okay, I like that. So, the linear combinations of the rows of *A* give you rows of *B*. And so, their span should be the same. So, row equivalent actually means we got from *A* to *B* using elementary row operations.

Again, Anne's strategic use of partner discussions prepared her students for a productive discussion. Anne's intentionality allowed her to elevate the status of women in her classroom and begin working toward a more gender-equitable environment.

Learning community session two

Looking at the data analytics for the second observation, there was an overall increase in student participation in whole-class discussions (from 16 to 23 contributions total). There was also greater variety in types of contributions, with *How* = 3, *What* = 13, *Why* = 2, and *Other* = 5. This indicates that students were providing contributions with more depth than the first observation. These trends are especially promising given that students spent more time in pairs (unlike in the first observation), yet there was still more and higher-quality whole-class discussion. During the debrief, Anne shared her intentionality in question types.

> I was more conscious of what types of questions I was asking, like following up on a "What?" with a "Why?"

Here Anne contrasts the *What*-level questions (asking for an answer) with deeper *Why*-level questions (asking for justification). Such questions are much more aligned with higher-order mathematics thinking.

Despite these broad improvements, participation remained skewed toward men, who had 1.1 average contributions while women only had 0.45. Anne was frustrated to see little change in this area, especially given her other areas of improvement.

> It really bothers me that this is so delineated along gender lines and other lines. [. . .] I want to understand this better.

Brian suggested that part of the reason for these inequities comes down to math trauma and how, for minoritized students, they have years of negative experiences from mathematics classrooms that are unaddressed.

Anne reflected on her increased awareness of *who* was participating and how hand raising played a role in improving that.

> [In prior class sessions,] I had people blurting things out, and it feels dynamic. But then I realized not everyone was blurting things out! So now everyone knows I'm waiting, but that does cause some awkwardness.

Here, Anne reflects on the awkwardness of trying a new strategy. She was accustomed to classroom environments in which students shouted out answers, but now she had to reckon with how that could exacerbate inequity. Similarly, Anne discussed how her first attempt to intentionally bring a woman into the discussion did not go so well, as the woman felt put on the spot and was unable to contribute successfully. These reflections highlight how learning takes time and instructors are likely to make mistakes along the way. However, with data documenting the impact of new strategies and a supportive learning community to sustain motivation, instructors are much more likely to continue to change in the face of such challenges.

Brian discussed the importance of framing to the students why they were being asked to participate. As a part of this discussion, Brian shared a resource from Stan Yoshinobu (from the Academy of Inquiry Based Learning) that talks about getting students to participate. Marie followed up with two concrete strategies. The first strategy was to explicitly ask students to respond to one another when asking questions. The second strategy was to use a quick partner discussion in response to student silence when a question is asked in the whole-class discussion, to provide more processing time. This allows the instructor to maintain the depth of their questioning without simplifying the question, as seen in Anne's first observation.

Observation three

Anne began the lesson with a brief check-in, asking students "What's your level of joy and contentment right now?" In addition to expressing her care for her students' well-being, it allowed her to gauge the classroom energy before diving into content. When Anne started the content of the lesson, she asked students what they knew about orthogonality, and a few students shouted out answers.

ANNE: What do you know about orthogonality?

MELODY [*not called on*]: It's perpendicular!

ANNE: Okay [*writes on the board*], that's a symbol for perpendicular. How can we tell whether two vectors are perpendicular?

[*Two women, Anita and Ashley, raise their hands immediately, and a couple seconds later one man in the back of the room raises his hand.*]

ANNE: Anita?

ANITA: The dot product.

ANNE: What do you do with the dot product?

ANITA: We see if it is equal to zero?

ANNE: Okay, Ashley, what were you going to say?

ASHLEY: [*Nodding head.*] The same thing. The dot product is equal to zero.

This episode illustrates Anne's use of the "multiple hands" strategy. Even after two women had raised their hand, Anne continued waiting, and eventually a third student raised their hand. After allowing this wait time, Anne provided both Anita and Ashley with opportunities to share. In this discussion, three of four participants were women, contrasting the first observation where women rarely spoke.

As the lesson continued, Anne posed a question about orthogonality to her class. After providing a long wait time (five seconds) without a response, Anne initiated a partner discussion. This was one of the strategies that Marie suggested during the last debrief meeting.

ANNE: I claim that these two vector spaces are orthogonal. Does anyone wanna tell me what that really means? [*Five seconds of silence.*]

ANNE: Okay, talk to your partner for a second, confer.

[*Students talking to each other loudly for about a minute.*]

ANNE: Okay, let's see what you got. Anyone want to finish this sentence? "Two vector spaces are orthogonal if . . ."

[*Anita raises a hand, Briana raises a hand, and another student raises a hand.*]

BRIANA: If the dot product of their bases is zero.

ANNE: Okay, let's write that down. But a basis has multiple things in that, so what do you mean by that?

BRIANA: That it's every basis vector.

ANNE: I'll write down what you said. That's a good idea, I think. Briana has a good idea. The dot product of bases equals zero. So do you think that the vector space of the floor is orthogonal or perpendicular to the vector space of these lines. Do you think so? Let's take a vote. How many people think yes?

[*Students raise hands.*]

Although Anne's initial question was met with silence, after providing partner time, multiple students raise their hands. When Briana contributes an idea, Anne presses for deeper explanation by asking "What do you mean?" She writes down Briana's idea and validates it as a "good idea" before soliciting a vote from the class.

As the lesson continued, Anne effectively used partner work to scaffold the whole-class discussion. Again, she used what she learned from student work time to intentionally bring in specific ideas to the discussion.

ANNE: Why don't you work on this problem too? [*Finding the basis for the image of* T *under some linear transformation.*]

[*Anne checks in with students working on the problem for about twelve minutes.*]

ANNE: Let's just go over this second problem. I really like what I heard over at Abigail and Nico's table, because they used language that we've been using in class.

ANNE: So, the image of *T*, is the set of, it lives in *R*-four, so it's gonna be the set *a*, *b*, *c*, *d*.

[*Anne continues working out the problem with participation from students.*]

ANNE: I think a lot of you nailed that puppy! Yes! A good place to start our weekend! [*Students applaud.*]

In this episode, Anne *assigns competence* to Abigail and Nico, validating their approach of using the language discussed in class. After highlighting this idea, Anne led the students to work out the problem, soliciting ideas from multiple students. This culminated with the students applauding themselves at the end of the lesson. This is a wonderful example of Anne's intentionality in bringing in students, deepening mathematical rigor, and building a strong sense of student community. All this became possible when Anne started to use a very small set of strategies she adopted from the learning community with great success.

Learning community session three

Participation in Anne's class continued to increase, with 29 contributions (the most yet). Again, there was a variety in types of contributions, with *How* = 7, *What* = 7, *Why* = 2, and *Other* = 13. In this lesson, there was a shift away from answers (*What* talk) toward discussing more processes and problem-solving steps (*How* talk). Most critically, Anne finally began to shift gendered patterns of participation. The average contributions from men were 1.1 and from women were 0.91. As the qualitative vignettes showed, women were volunteering and actively contributed to the discussions.

During this debrief, Anne discussed some of her strategies for framing the importance of participation to her students (following up on Brian's suggestion from the second debrief). All these events took place before the third observed lesson.

First, Anne shared her experiences playing in an orchestra and told her students how it was important for her to move around, interact with different people, and listen to the music from different places on the stage. During this conversation, Anne intentionally made "eye contact with the women." Later, she followed up on that conversation during office hours, talking to women in her classroom in a one-on-one setting.

Second, Anne created an activity for students to practice moving around the room and interacting with others. She treated the classroom like a physical grid, using matrix notation to refer to specific student chairs as parts of different rows and columns. This was seamless integration of both mathematical and social goals (i.e., understanding the notation and talking with peers). Anne shared that in the past she would've been reticent to do such an activity because she was afraid to make students uncomfortable. The support of the learning community made this possible for her.

Third, Anne created an activity around what she called the *Long Theorem* (also called the Invertible Matrix Theorem). This theorem is a list of twenty-three equivalent statements, each related to whether an n by n matrix is invertible.

> I cut each statement on a piece of paper. They each got a paper. Whoever they were sitting next to, they had to prove the other person's statement from theirs. And then they wrote it on the blackboard. I noticed that people who never talked in class got up and wrote up really nice answers. So I could say, "That's a really nice answer."

Fourth, Anne and her class developed a two-voices rule, to alternate who spoke in the class.

> We tried a wait-two-voices rule. So, if you say something, you have to wait until two other people talk before you talk again.

Together, these examples show how the suggestions from her coaching team empowered her to experiment with new ideas that she previously would've been reticent to try. Anne further reflected on how some of the practices she learned had now become staples in her repertoire, such as a turn-and-talk.

> I've used that a lot. Or I have a vote, and if nobody votes, I say "Okay, we have to talk about that." It's a new habit. I didn't use this "talk to each other and come back" [strategy] previously.

The "talk to each other and come back" strategy was perhaps the single most important strategy that Anne used because it allowed her to learn more about her students and intentionally elevate the status of women in her classroom.

Observation four

During the fourth observation, Anne was teaching about eigenvectors. Anne continued to use strategies from the prior observations, so here I only provide brief snippets of her practice. For example, Anne continued to press students to explain their ideas, as in the following episode.

ANNE: If I have matrix times nonzero vector equals zero, what do I know about the determinant of this matrix?

HANK: It should be zero because it's not invertible.

ANNE: The determinant has to be zero, Hank says, because it's not invertible. Why is that not invertible? Maya, do you agree with that? How do I know it's not invertible? It doesn't say that on there.

MAYA: If it were invertible, then the only vector that would work for it to equal zero would be the zero vector.

ANNE: Because? For it to be invertible it has to be?

MAYA: One-to-one.

Here, Anne receives a response from Hank and uses it as an opportunity to both invite Maya into the discussion and press for deeper thinking. These types of higher-level facilitation strategies were not something that Anne used before her work in the learning community.

Anne continued to move between partner work and whole-class discussions to foster deeper conversations. For example, in the following episode, Anne posed a problem for the students to find eigenvalues for a two-by-two matrix and intentionally selected a student to present at the board.

ANNE: Now I know that if I can find lambdas that make that equal to zero, then those lambdas will be eigenvalues. So go ahead and work that out, and tell me what you get.

[*Student work time: Anne circulates the room and walks over and talks with Amelia.*]

ANNE: All right, Amelia's got it here; she's gonna write it up on the board for us.

AMELIA: [*Writing solution on the board.*] Sorry it's so messy, but it's there.

ANNE: So, we have two eigenvalues, does that surprise you? No. In fact, if you have a two-by-two matrix and you put lambdas and find the determinant, you'll always have a quadratic, so you expect no more than two eigenvalues.

Writing a solution at the board can be an intimating experience for students, as implied by Amelia's comment ("Sorry it's so messy"). Simultaneously, Anne has done considerable work to make this a safer experience. By conferring with Amelia in a one-on-one setting and then confirming her solution is correct, she creates space for Amelia to be seen as publicly competent as she writes up on the board. Over time, the culmination of episodes such as this one created a classroom environment that cherished the brilliance of women in mathematics.

Learning community session four

Anne's fourth observation had a total of 22 contributions in whole-class discussions, with *How* = 1, *What* = 8, *Why* = 7, and *Other* = 6. Of all observed lessons, this one had the most explanations (*why*-level talk). It also had the highest proportion of average contributions from women (1.36) compared to the proportion from men (0.41). These findings are truly remarkable. Anne's intentional use of strategies over the semester, supported by data and just three prior debrief meetings, allowed her to transform the gender dynamics of her classroom.

Rather than focusing on new teaching strategies, the final debrief was more celebratory in nature. Anne and Ramesh, the other faculty member in Anne's community, reflected more broadly on gender dynamics they've seen in higher education. They also spent time talking with the coaching team and sharing gratitude for their learning across the semester.

SUMMARY AND REFLECTIONS

Anne's participation in an equity learning community was in response to a voluntary solicitation, and her focus was guided by her own personal and professional goals. The intake interview was used to uncover her focus on gender inequity and understand what strategies she had tried in the past (e.g., random calling) and whether she had any concrete strategies. Given that Anne had her own concrete experiences of gender marginalization, there was less of a need to focus on building empathy for women in her classes, and instead, to focus on helping her develop concrete strategies. As the equity learning community cycles clearly demonstrate, Anne made concrete changes to her teaching with measurable impacts on the quality and distribution of classroom participation. Here I provide summary visualizations and instructor reflections on the process.

Figure 2.1 shows the trends in average contributions across observations (with approximately three weeks between each observation). Overall, there was an upward trend in total student contributions, and proportionally, more of these contributions were from women. Although there was some drop in participation from men during the final session, a single observation should be interpreted cautiously in the context of overall trends in the data. Thus, I would argue that while participation from men may have reduced near the end of the semester, there is insufficient evidence to back that claim.

The amazing thing about Anne's story is that even as a woman who was a successful mathematician and dedicated to promoting women in mathematics, these commitments were not evident in the first (baseline) observation, which shows stark gender inequities. However, when Anne was immersed in a supportive community, provided with meaningful data, and instructed to adopt specific teaching moves, she made impressive changes to her teaching practice and to gender equity. Although Anne experimented with a variety of teaching moves, there were four primary moves that shifted her repertoire of practice.

1. Framing the importance of participation to students, both through discussions and concrete activities (e.g., desks as rows and columns, proving the Long Theorem).
2. Requiring students to raise their hands rather than shouting out answers, and waiting for multiple students to raise their hands before calling on someone.

FIGURE 2.1 Average contributions by gender in Anne's class during the Fall 2021 semester

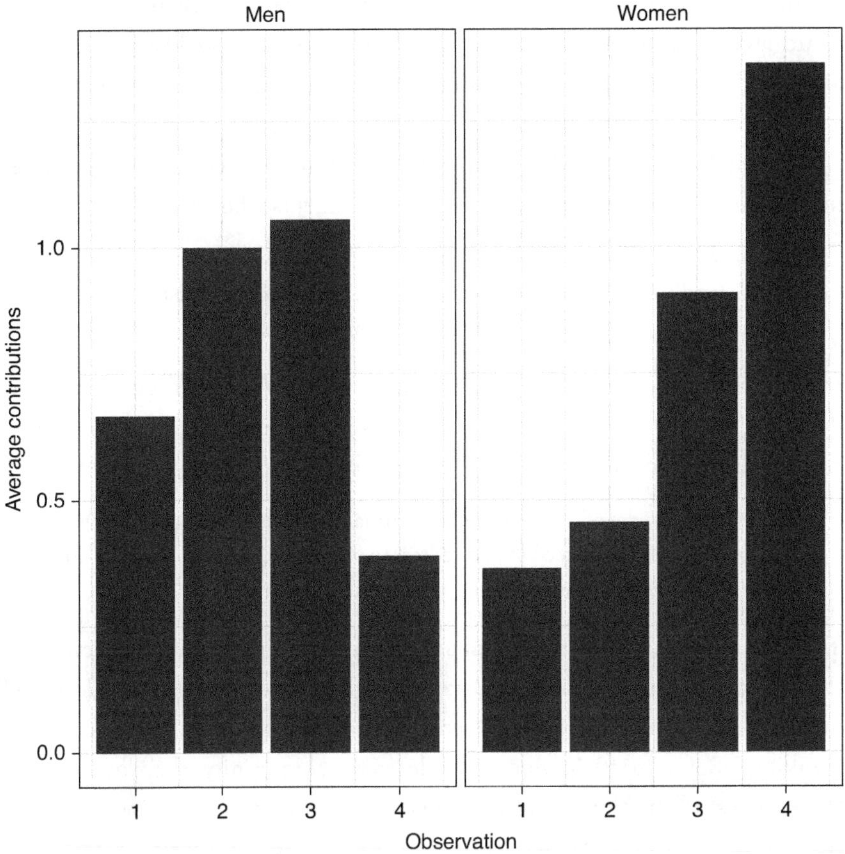

3. Asking questions that required deeper thinking (i.e., *Why* versus *What*), and probing students to respond more deeply.
4. Intentionally selecting minoritized students during partner-work time to later share out during the whole-class discussion and elevate their ideas publicly.

Notably, these strategies were not a complete overhaul of Anne's teaching style. They were small but powerful instructional moves that she integrated across her lessons. Over time, she learned to integrate the strategies more often and more effectively. These strategies are so simple and productive that *all* instructors should be using them. I have personally seen their benefit across a wide variety of instructional settings, and they have been used as foundational levers for change within equity learning communities, both for Anne and others. While these strategies can be effective in general, Anne's use of data allowed her to intentionally bring in specific students to redress gender inequities in her classroom. Data allow for intentionality.

Anne reflected on how the equity learning community helped her build awareness of participation dynamics, especially for students who are quiet.

> We're always really aware of the people that talk a lot. But the people who don't talk, it's for different reasons. And maybe, I think the first step is just being aware, and that's what this whole videotaping thing made me do.

In addition to becoming aware of the students who were not participating, Anne developed greater awareness of the students who were dominating and how that could create a space that was less welcoming for others.

> I'm a lot more aware of the people who dominate and, then, how that makes the other people feel. I've learned to just address that head-on. We're going to let other people share the air. I know that it's important, so I just do that.

To make sense of why some students were not participating, Anne drew upon the idea of "math trauma" that Brian brought up during the second debrief meeting. This made Anne more "sensitive to people who are traumatized by speaking." Before participating in the learning community, she would simply leave these students alone and let them be quiet because she didn't want to force them to participate. Now, she had a new perspective and specific strategies to involve those students in the discussion.

> Acknowledging that some students may have a hard time sharing their views because of their prior trauma, or whatever the reason might be, I've learned some strategies. One of them is to have students talk to each other and then walk around and listen for when someone has a good idea. Then I'll say, "Elayne had that idea, and Sarah has this good idea; do you want to share?" That gives them the courage to share, and it really works. And it also works for me, that practice of listening to everyone to see what their ideas are.

This strategy of using partner-work time to intentionally bring students into the whole-class was the fourth strategy listed above. Arguably, alongside having students raise their hand, this was the single most important change that Anne made to her instruction. Anne also used this strategy to address silence in response to a question she asked, which allowed her to broader participation and maintain high levels of academic rigor.

> If nobody's voting, then I say, "It seems like you're unsure, so why don't you talk to each other, and I'll give you a few minutes to make up your minds." And then they do vote, and then they do participate.

Figure 2.2 provides an example of that academic rigor. As highlighted in her learning cycles, over time, Anne was able to incorporate deeper contributions from her students (*Why* versus *What*). Figure 2.2 illustrates that Anne was able to

FIGURE 2.2 Student talk types by gender in Anne's class during the Fall 2021 semester

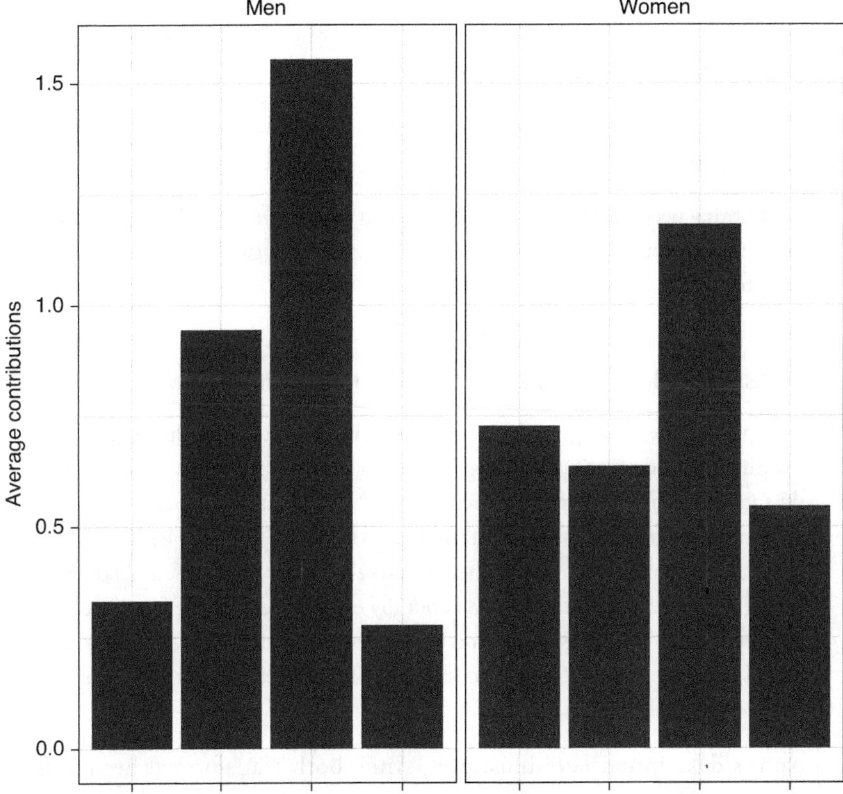

enhance this depth and still do so in an equitable way. In fact, the highest levels contributions (*Why* and *How*), came primarily from women! This is notable because in some equity efforts, to broaden participation, instructors offer low-level contributions broadly but reserve the most meaningful contributions for their positively stereotyped students.

During her exit interview, a whole year after her participation in the learning community, Anne shared some of her lasting takeaways. Anne discussed how the data made this possible by creating greater awareness of which students were dominating her conversations.

> For me, the data were huge. I had no idea; that first observation, it was so clear that most people were saying nothing, especially women. And two guys were talking all the time. Sometimes you know someone is talking a lot, but really, that's quite bad. That made a huge impression for me. Really the data was the biggest thing. Otherwise, it's just how we feel at the end of class, and that's affected by so many things like who comes to your office hours.

Given how much she valued the experience, Anne was interested in ways to share it with her colleagues.

> My burning need, really, is for information that I got from these meetings; mostly Brian was the source of wisdom. I feel like if we could just get more people to learn this stuff [it would have a huge impact].

One way that Anne attempted to share her learning was by running a departmental workshop for her colleagues in the year following her year of participation.

> As a part of the visiting professor, I just taught one class, and the expectation was that I would contribute the department in enriching ways. [. . .] I wanted to do something on participation, because I had been thinking about it so much. So, I made up a workshop and I started out with calling on people. It could be that I have a spinner. [. . .] And then we talked about how that felt. And challenges that they had. Then I talked about my experience with the [equity learning community] and how I was kind of shocked and validated by looking at the actual data, the things I tried, and so forth. Then I tried to get them to reflect on their own teaching.

As Anne's description here illustrates, Anne both transformed her teaching and became an advocate for others to transform their teaching. Beyond teaching, Anne also discussed how her notion of participation expanded beyond the classroom.

> This idea of participation, in my head, has expanded outside of the classroom into who do I ask to be a grader or mentor and help play these roles. I realize that the strengths that people have in explaining or talking or articulating may not be loud; they may be soft. I have thought a lot more about that. If I look at which students are working for me now, they look different from a year ago.

As Anne's story makes clear, the impact and potential from an equity learning community was profound. Anne's progress within the single semester outlined above is truly impressive and underscores the possibilities for this work to transform education.

KEY TAKEAWAYS

Anne's case highlights many of the important features of an equity learning community and provides a blueprint for others who would use the method. Here I summarize two key takeaways and connect them to coaching work.

Data increase motivation and capacity for change. Despite a long and successful career working toward gender equity in mathematics, the initial impact of seeing classroom data was profound for Anne. It created a greater sense of urgency for Anne to adjust her teaching practices to reduce inequities. She described having data as the "biggest thing" to move beyond gut impressions and to address gender inequities. Because gut impressions are subject to bias, the data provided a much more objective benchmark for progress.

Anne showed some initial skepticism of the strategies that were suggested (e.g., having students raise their hands felt awkward), and initially, they did not always go as planned (e.g., little change in gendered participation patterns and an awkward experience trying to bring a woman into the conversations). Despite these bumps in the road, by the third observation, the data showed evidence of positive impact due to new teaching strategies. This provided greater motivation and excitement for Anne, who found deeper value in the work and continued to experiment with new strategies. This is a common shift that we have seen in equity learning communities. Instructors may have initial reticence to use unfamiliar teaching methods, but once they experiment with new methods *and* receive data showing a positive impact, it becomes a positive feedback loop that produces further changes. From a coaching perspective, it's important to provide support that allows for risk-taking, especially in the beginning, which is later bolstered by empirical data documenting the impact of instructional changes.

Incremental changes accumulate to a larger impact. As the chapter title suggests, Anne's story is an exemplar of incremental change. This a cornerstone of equity learning communities. Incremental change allowed Anne to move from a classroom in which men dominated discussions to one in which women actively volunteered their insights. Even more powerfully, the empirical data were rich enough that improvements in gender equity could be *directly* tied to specific teaching moves, like intentionally highlighting the ideas of women that emerged during partner work.

On one hand, it's remarkable how much Anne's classroom changed. Simultaneously, it's remarkable that she only made modest changes to her overall teaching approach. Anne used four primary strategies regularly and effectively—framing conversations around participation, waiting for multiple hands, deepening student reasoning, and using partner work to support whole-class discussions. Although the strategies began to manifest regularly in her facilitation—especially hand raising, questioning strategies, and intentionally highlighting students—the bulk of her lessons had not changed. Lessons still featured a large amount of instructor-driven talk, used real-world examples, and prized mathematical rigor.

These four strategies are relatively easy to learn and are go-to strategies for coaches building their own communities. This case highlights how coaches do not need to be experts in everything education related, and they don't need to prescribe radical instructional change to see an impact. Rather, coaches can focus on just a few high-leverage practices that are relatively easy to use and guide instructors in using them to intentionally support students from minoritized social-marker groups.

CHAPTER 3

Gwen's Story: Shifting Perspectives and Shifting Instruction

The instructional shifts that result from an equity learning community can also shift instructors' perspectives about equity. We saw an example of this already in the previous chapter, as Anne used "math trauma" as a lens to make sense of students who were not participating in her class. In this chapter, I explore Gwen's story, which provides a deeper look at how instructor perspectives can shift throughout the course of an equity learning community. Again, I highlight two key takeaways in this chapter.

Equitable teaching supports specific students. Gwen was a highly experienced mathematics educator with extensive practice collaboratively engaging her students in small groups and discussions. Although these teaching moves are often framed as "equitable teaching moves" in the literature, the key element that was missing from her practice was using these strategies with intentionality. Specifically, Gwen needed to learn how to use instructional strategies to support specific students (often based on social-marker identities) to elevate their status and engagement. Empirical data across the semester document improvements in gender equity and some improvements in racial equity, with slightly mixed results for Black students.

Instructor perspectives and practices can shift together. A key theme of the chapter is how Gwen's conceptions of equity shifted and how that impacted her teaching practices. Across learning community cycles, Gwen continued to reflect on her understanding of equity, slowly moving toward a conceptualization that incorporated historical inequities as an important factor in considering how to intentionally support students in her classroom.

Gwen participated in an equity learning community for two semesters (teaching in person), with one other faculty participant, coach Kelly (described in a later chapter), and student coder Jerome. Here, I focus on the first semester of participation to illustrate Gwen's learning process in depth and show what is possible within just four debrief meetings over a semester. Like Anne's case, explored in the previous chapter, Gwen's case is notable: She is a woman of color in mathematics who actively advocated for racial and gender equity but still needed concrete teaching practices to enact her vision in her classroom. In this chapter, I provide a brief overview of Gwen's background, work through her four reflection cycles in the learning community, discuss her reflections on the process, and highlight key takeaways.

GWEN'S PROFILE

Gwen is an Asian American woman and tenured professor of mathematics education at a private university. Gwen described her pedagogy as actively engaging students with group work and whole-class discussions. She typically let students group themselves but also used random grouping strategies to help students get to know each other. During the fall 2021 semester, Gwen was teaching *Mathematics and Society*, an undergraduate course for non-math majors. This course focused on a variety of equity-focused issues, like critical race theory, achievement gaps and tracking, and gerrymandering. This was an in-person course, but during some sessions, Gwen allowed one to two students to participate over Zoom in a hybrid format. The demographics of Gwen's class are given in table 3.1.

During her intake interview, Gwen articulated an equity goal of providing all students with appropriate support to reach the same level of understanding (i.e.,

TABLE 3.1 Demographics in Gwen's class (fall 2021, in person)

		Race/Ethnicity			
		Black	Latine	Mixed	**Total**
Gender	Man	0	0	3	3
	Woman	2	8	1	11
	Total	2	8	4	14

Note: All students in the mixed category were mixed-white.

equal output, different support). Rather than forcing quiet students to participate, such as through cold calling, Gwen engaged them in other ways, like office hours and one-on-one check-ins. As an Asian American woman, she had experienced stereotyping, and for her, she saw race and gender as closely linked. Consequently, she was mindful of student differences and focused on using inclusive language in her teaching.

REFLECTION CYCLES

Here I outline the set of observations of Gwen's teaching and her revisions to practice over time.

Observation one

Gwen was teaching in a collaborative-learning space with students seated at tables in four different small groups. During her first observed class session, students started by discussing a homework reading on critical race theory. Her instruction was organized between cycles of small-group discussions at the tables (during which Gwen would move around the room and check in with students) and whole-class debriefs. Gwen provided wait time and consistently checked with students for understanding. During debriefs, Gwen solicited participation with phrases like "Let's go around and have every group share." While this distributed participation *across* groups, Gwen did not yet use strategies to select students *within* groups.

Although Gwen's students participated readily, the discussion was mostly dominated by the three men in the class (and two men in specific, Luca and Elia). For example, after Gwen invited the four groups to share responses to the assigned homework reading, in 3 of 4 cases, men were the ones who shared out. Thus, while men were only 3 of 14 students in the class, in this discussion, 3 of 4 contributions were from men. The only time that a woman responded was in a group that consisted of only women.

Gwen offered students a variety of supports for participation. To begin, she made norms of engagement explicit for students, using language as follows:

GWEN: There's different ways to work in groups with each other. I know last time people were breaking up questions and assigning "You do this question, you do this question, and you do this question." That is a way to manage and break

> up the work. But what I would like to achieve is for you all to deepen your understanding of the papers by discussing the guiding questions. So, these questions are to guide you to have a discussion [together].

When Gwen asked questions to the whole class and students were quiet, she would give them a short amount of time to discuss in their groups before coming back to the whole class and allowing students to volunteer. She also explicitly asked for new students to participate using language like "This time maybe we can have somebody else share?" Although Gwen attempted to solicit participation from a variety of students, most of the time, students would share their responses without raising their hands or being called on. When they did raise their hands, she typically called on the very first student who raised their hand.

After checking in with a variety of student groups, Gwen realized that not everyone had a strong grasp of what critical race theory was. She used this as the basis for a classroom discussion to build common understanding among her students.

GWEN: Let's try that again. What is critical race theory?

LUCA: It tells us how racism impacts outcomes and experiences.

GWEN: Okay, so not just race, but racism. I don't know, what is the difference between race and racism?

LUCA: Racism is mean, so [*everyone laughs*].

GWEN: Good, so that's a description of the impact.

ELSA: It's the discrimination and bias against certain groups based on their race.

GWEN: Okay, discrimination based on their race. And what is race?

AKIRA: The grouping of humans based on shared physical or social qualities, with the categories generally being viewed as distinct by society.

GWEN: Interesting, okay. Okay, one thing I would add to that. Luca, you want to add to that?

LUCA: I was gonna say it's a social construct to group people.

GWEN: Yeah, that's what I was gonna say. [. . .] For me as a child of immigrants, I'm the same race as my parents, but we have very different cultural experiences. So yeah, anyways. So critical race theory is a framework, it is a lens, to look at a situation, whether it is in court, and now it has branched to education. It is looking at what happens in the classroom. Who gets sent to the principal's office more often than others? Instead of saying they are just taking a blind look at it and "they are bad, so they are sent to the principal's office," let's take a look, let's take a look at the actions.

ELIA: So basically, we're just looking at education, but it could be used for any situation?

GWEN: Yes, so Elia's saying, okay, but could this also be approached in a restaurant or in the mall? It's like any situation where there is a human, there are social dynamics. I mean, you can see it in movies, even when you watch movies. So, it's a lens through which to look at the world. The word *lens* comes from a camera. You can change lenses to see things differently. I have a macro lens that can look at something really close, and then I have a telescope lens that means I can see something really far. So it's just another lens to look at the world.

LUCA: This stems from like laws, which are supposed to look at the world objectively, but I feel like race and racism creates a certain bias. And then this theory tries to make it objective again?

GWEN: Actually, I think it's the other way. Do you hear what Luca is saying?

Throughout the discussion, a variety of students participated, but the three dominant participants were mixed-race (half-White) men (Akira, Elia, and Luca).[1] There was minimal participation from Black and Latine students, even though Gwen was trying to create a space that explicitly acknowledged racism and racial inequity. After this discussion, Gwen broke the students into groups to discuss for about fifteen more minutes. At the close of the lesson, Gwen shared how she appreciated the student participation and how she was initially nervous to have these conversations in her classroom. This was an example of Gwen showing vulnerability to support her students to do the same.

GWEN: I thought I was going to have such a hard time talking about race with you all, but it's actually not as hard as I thought. I was scared. I really appreciate how you have courage to have these conversations.

Overall, Gwen used a lot of advanced facilitation strategies to create norms, build a comfortable space, and support her students to engage. This was reflective of her background and training in mathematics education.

Learning community session one

During the initial community session, the group spent a fair amount of time checking in, introducing themselves, and getting to know one another. This approach reflected coach Kelly's orientation to building positive group dynamics. After checking in, Jerome provided both participants with data analytics describing their classroom participation.

During Gwen's first observed lesson, there were 41 contributions, with *What* = 26, *Why* = 10, and *Other* = 5. This shows that Gwen was already engaging students to explain their thinking with *Why* discourse. Because Gwen was already engaging students at deeper levels, this was not an area of focus throughout the semester, so I will not report on it for future lessons, instead focusing on gender and race breakdowns of engagement.

The gender breakdown was seventeen men (41 percent) and twenty-four women (58 percent). Given that women made up almost 80 percent of the class demographics, this was 5.66 average contributions for men and only 2.18 average contributions for women. Additionally, in the initial observation, more than half of the contributions came from multiracial (mixed-White) students, who only made up 35 percent of the classroom demographics. Thus, average contributions by race were mixed-White = 4.5, Latine = 2, and Black = 3.5. Jerome noted that three students dominated—Elia, Luca, and Akira—and together, those three had more contributions than all other students combined. These three mixed-White men were the ones who dominated the public conversational space.

The juxtaposition of Gwen's initial observation and her preliminary data analytics may be surprising. As a mathematics educator who was implementing a wide variety of effective practices for supporting classroom discourse (e.g., building norms, inviting students to participate, checking for understanding, fostering relationships, and using positive discourse moves, wait time, and group work), one might expect that the data would be more equitable. However, the missing element was intentionality with these strategies to support students based on social-marker identities. Although a diverse array of high-quality participation opportunities were being created, unless those are distributed equitably, the resulting participation patterns could still be inequitable.

Although there were marked inequities in participation, this learning community session didn't focus on specific interventions to alleviate such inequities. Rather, it focused on community building to teach students to self-monitor participation, as evident in Kelly's suggestion.

> One community norm that my students would come up with often was "take space, make space" so they would be more conscious of the space that they take and the space that they make. [. . .] When you're hesitant to answer a question, do you want to say pass? How many times do you want to say pass before you're asked to share? As a class, they make up these norms for the community, so when they are in a discussion, they can help each other.

Kelly's suggestion around building community norms was to create a space in which students could support one another (and hold one another accountable) to have more equitable participation. Although she didn't use this exact norm, in her second observation, Gwen did emphasize a norm of "step forward, step back," which is similar in intent.

The community also discussed student check-ins. Gwen expressed her struggles with checking in with students around social justice issues, which felt more difficult than checking in about math problems. Kelly responded with strategies she used to check in as a counselor.

> In the beginning of my class, I typically have a check-in that is thumbs up, in the middle, thumbs down, how are we feeling today, how is the week going? It's not related to content. One week I had a check-in to find an ice cream flavor of how you're feeling right now. It sounds weird, but it's a safe question, because you're not asking the deep question of "Did you have any struggles today," but you're giving them a way to share like "rocky road," and you can follow up, "What did you mean by rocky road?" And someone else might have "rocky road" that they share as well, so they can relate to each other about how they are experiencing their week or the class content, because I've also asked how are we feeling about the class?

In future observations, Gwen adopted this strategy to integrate more check-ins into her course.

Finally, the community discussed the meaning of equity. Gwen shared her initial model of encouraging but not forcing students who were uncomfortable to participate. Kelly responded by framing an equitable classroom as one in which all students would feel comfortable to share. Gwen responded that this was a new idea for her.

> You said equity to you means comfort enough to share in the classroom, and I hadn't thought about it like that. I think that's maybe equity in the classroom. [. . .] I liked hearing your definition.

This conversation marked the beginning of Gwen's shift in perspective about equity. As the conversations above illustrate, the nature of Gwen's learning community differed from Anne's. The focus was less on concrete strategies and more about reflection, processing, and understanding.

Observation two

Gwen's teaching style continued to alternate between small-group and whole-class discussions. As suggested during the prior learning community session, Gwen used a check-in to assess student understanding on a homework problem that involved interpretation of a graph of racial disparities in responses to emails sent to businesses.

GWEN: Remember how on Zoom I did a temperature check? Let's do a visual temperature check. One is "I still need time to process, I don't understand this yet," and ten is "You can give me a quiz on this, I get it." Can you just hold up fingers so I can get a visual of where the class is? And that will help me say "Let's spend time more time on this" or "Okay, let's move on." Both ways are good for me, but I don't know unless I hear from you. So, can you all hold up fingers? [. . .] Thank you very much for your feedback. So, there are quite a bit that are five and under, so I would like to spend a little bit more time to discuss this. The people who put five and under, can I invite you to ask a question that might make interpreting this graph a bit easier? And I'll give you some time to think of that question.

As this episode shows, Gwen used a check-in to assess her students' understanding and then invited students to ask questions. Gwen's framing was that "both ways are good for me, but I won't know unless I hear from you." This created space for students to share how they were struggling with the problems.

LISA: I had a question on the assignment. For one of the questions, you asked what was the largest gap that favored White males? And I put businesses here. Do you want me to explain why businesses has the largest gap or how I know it is?

GWEN: Both. In the beginning [of the assignment] I highlighted, support all your answers.

ELIA: I'm looking at the business one. Does 62 percent plus 20 percent mean that 82 percent of people got a response?

GWEN: 82 percent of White males got a response.

ELIA: And 20 percent of them, that's what I'm confused about. Where does that come from?

GWEN: Okay, that's a good question. Elia has a question. What does this 20 percent on the bar actually mean? Can somebody in the class help out? Remember, step forward, and step back. What does this 20 percent represent? Maybe someone who hasn't spoken yet today? You all have done really well so far on the stepping forward and stepping back. I notice it. Can anyone help with Elia's question, what does that 20 percent, that gray bar, represent? [*Waits about five seconds.*]

KRISS: The 20 percent is the gap between women and minorities to the White men, right?

GWEN: What do you think Elia?

ELIA: I was thinking, Is the 20 percent like the ones that got like the bad email address?

GWEN: Oh, they don't ask whether it's bad or not, they just count whether it's a response or not. Luca?

LUCA: Those bars don't actually correspond to anything, they are just the differences between two percentages. They don't represent like a certain type of email they got or something. It is just saying that minorities got 62 percent and White males got 82 percent, and there's a 20 percent difference.

GWEN: I like the word you used there, *difference*. Difference; what do you think Elia? What do you think of Luca's response?

ELIA: So, you're saying it doesn't represent anything?

LUCA: It just says White males got 20 percent more responses. It shows how much more White males got.

ELIA: So, they got more responses than the minorities?

LUCA: Yeah.

GWEN: Hold on, Elissa, you were nodding. Why?

ELISSA: I said we were just adding. So, you start with 62 percent, and you're adding 20 percent to 62 percent to show that they were favored more.

GWEN: Does that make sense to everybody?

In this episode, Gwen reminds the students of the norm "step up and step back," invites someone to speak who hasn't spoken yet, and supports students to respond to one another. Despite these instructional strategies, Gwen was still not explicitly moderating *who* participated in the discussion, and both Elia and Luca were main contributors to the discussion. This highlights a general pattern I have noticed across classrooms. Although instructors can invite students to self-monitor their participation, dominant students tend to do a poor job of this and continue to dominate anyway. For this reason, it is essential for instructors to use explicit strategies to mediate who talks (e.g., five hands and intentionally selecting students after group work time).

In the episode, Gwen more directly invited students to participate in the discussion. She first calls on Leyli by name and then solicits voices from each of the groups.

GWEN: Based on this table, how many of those emails were responded to by the faculty? Uh, Leyli?

LEYLI: Uh [*hesitates and pauses*].

GWEN: You can say pass. Maybe I should say the question again. If one hundred emails were sent with either a minority or person of color with their name on it, one hundred of those emails were sent out to businesses, how many emails were responded to? Someone in this group?

FIONA: sixty-two?

GWEN: Sixty-two. Do you agree? Okay, so now let's suppose one hundred emails were sent with White male's names, were sent to businesses. How many emails were responded to? Maybe someone from this group? Did you all speak already? This group then?

LUCA AND KRISS: Eighty-two.

GWEN: So, you both say eighty-two. How do you know that? Can you explain, Kriss?

KRISS: [*Inaudible response.*]

GWEN: Did you all hear that over here? Okay, now what percentage of the White males got a response by the engineering and computer science department? Discuss in your groups and come up with an answer. [. . .] Let's go around to each group and have everyone explain how they got their answer.

Gwen uses some productive strategies here. When Leyli feels uncomfortable responding to the question, she gives her a "pass" to participate later. She also goes to each group for an explanation. Further, when both Luca and Kriss responded to a question, Gwen lets Kriss (a Black woman) elaborate rather than Luca (a dominant mixed-White man). Although Gwen was beginning to moderate student participation, there were still opportunities for her to take up simple and explicit teaching moves to do so more directly. For example, Gwen could've checked in with Leyli before the whole-class debrief to provide think time, or she could've selected specific students from the groups to share out. We see this suggestion offered during the next debrief.

Learning community session two

Kelly began the meeting with a check-in, asking for one thing that is going well and one thing that could be going better. Gwen responded that it was going okay, but she felt like the students have started to talk less as the semester goes on. However, in contrast to Gwen's perception, there was an increase in coded contributions. In total there were forty-four contributions, and twelve of the fourteen students participated. It's possible the observed lesson was an anomaly or that Gwen's perceptions were related to how she had intentionally slowed down her class sessions. By gender, average contributions were women = 2.45 and men = 5.66. By race, average contributions were Black = 1.5, Latine = 2.5, and mixed-White = 5.25. Although there was a slight increase in participation by women, racial inequity remained nearly the same.

Gwen mentioned two shifts she had made. First, she stopped asking "Do you have any questions?" and started asking, "What questions do you have?" Second, she talked about how she was encouraging specific students to participate.

> I want [the students] to be reflective on their own participation. I want them to pay attention to whether they have spoken or not. Overall, I think they are pretty good at it. They are pretty good at saying "Okay, you should speak."

> There are a couple of students I've really been trying to get to speak more—Leah and Aileen—and they have been talking so much more within their groups. Before it was nothing, and now it's like within their groups. And I'm seeing, Aileen especially, she was talking a lot in her group, and then I witnessed her stepping back. I have a norm "step forward, step back." So, she stepped back and said to Leyli "Oh, would you also like to share?" So, I want them to evaluate their own behavior. I think we can transfer that to other situations.

Notably, Leah and Aileen did both increase their participation in observation two, from zero public contributions to one for Aileen, and from one to four public contributions for Leah. These data suggest that Gwen's explicit attention to supporting these students had an impact.

Despite some progress, Jerome noticed that even when Gwen would ask for new students to participate, the same students would speak up again. Jerome suggested that Gwen predetermine who would share out after group time, using language like "When we come back, the student whose birthday is coming up next can share." Because students would be chosen ahead of time, it would avoid the same students volunteering repeatedly, but it would also provide preparation time, making it different from a cold call. Gwen committed to trying this strategy.

Observation three

Gwen started this lesson with a brief student presentation, and shortly thereafter broke students up into groups for group work time. When students came back from work time, she tried Jerome's strategy for predetermined contributions.

GWEN: We're gonna have one person from each group share, and the person who is gonna share is the person who is the youngest in the group.

[*Students talking to each other about their birthdays.*]

GWEN: Let's start with this group over here; so who is gonna share something you learned, to review gerrymandering?

ELSA: Um, there was cracking and packing.

GWEN: Cool, do you remember what cracking and packing were?

ELSA: If I remember correctly, cracking is spreading out the certain party. [. . .]

GWEN: Are we all [. . .] I wanna remind us of our norms, "be present" and "step forward, step back." So cracking is which one?

ELSA: Spreading out voters from different groups.

GWEN: Other groups, What do we think?

LISA: Is it by like changing district lines?

GWEN: All right, yes, but I also want to go back to the cracking bit. Cracking different groups into different districts. Are we all okay with that? And packing is?

ELSA: Packing is putting like [*laughs*] putting groups together.

GWEN: Did you wanna add something to that Luca?

LUCA: [*Inaudible.*]

As this episode shows, Gwen's strategy brought Elsa and Lisa, who were rarely involved in previous observations, into the conversation. Nonetheless, Gwen didn't fully implement the strategy because she told students who would share out *after* the discussion time rather than *before*, which provided less preparation time (although she remedied this when she used the strategy later in the lesson). Gwen continued to go across the groups and even invited the students who were on Zoom (some class sessions were hybrid).

GWEN: And this group?

LEONNA: We said splitting up the districts in a way that benefits a specific political party.

GWEN: Ah, good, okay. So together we have splitting up districts in a way that benefits one party. We do that by cracking or packing. Jordan, do you have anything to add?

JORDAN [ON ZOOM CHAT]: There are districts and precincts.

Overall, given that most students in the class were women, the strategy of preselecting students had a positive impact on reducing gendered inequities. Also, because many of the women were Black or Latine, it also reduced racial disparities in participation. Gwen used the same strategy again to debrief later in the lesson, but this time she predetermined the students *before* the discussion, allowing for more preparation time.

GWEN: Okay, second takeaway. First takeaway is the eldest child in the family. I guess let's do the second takeaway will be the youngest child in the family. So, what was it?

LUCA: If an efficiency gap is 8 percent or higher, then usually it is bad.

GWEN: If efficiency gap is greater than 8 percent, then what does *bad* mean?

LUCA: Uh, like it shouldn't be, like they shouldn't be considered [*pauses*].
[*Multiple students answering with overlapping, inaudible speech.*]
GWEN: Wait, sorry. Okay, something wrong, yes, Leyli.
LEYLI: I'm guessing there was, like there's something wrong with the votes.
LUCA: Rigged.
GWEN: Something wrong, something rigged; Leah, you were saying something?
LEAH: Fixed, so like the vote. [. . .]
GWEN: So, what is fixed?
KAITLYN: Sabotaged.
LUCA: Gerrymandering is wrong.

This episode shows that the strategy of predetermining students was partially effective. It did bring in new voices to the discussion. At the same time, by random chance, it still brought in dominant voices (like Luca). After Luca offered that an 8 percent efficiency gap was "bad," multiple students spoke up at the same time, and Gwen intentionally selected Leyli (a typically quiet student) to share her answer more clearly. In another instance, Breeann shouted out "sabotaged," even though when Gwen returned to her to elaborate, she declined to do so. Although Gwen did bring more students into the conversation, Luca continued to shout out ideas and dominate in the conversation.

Learning community session three

Gwen's strategy of preselecting students to present was partially successful. More students shared their ideas, and it did have an impact on the distribution of participation. By gender, average contributions were women = 3.55 and men = 4.33. This was the first time that gender dynamics began to shift. By race, average contributions were Black = 4.5, Latine = 3.25, and mixed-White = 4.25. Again, this was the first time that racialized participation patterns began to shift.

Gwen continued to ponder what classroom equity meant. Because this question was in the forefront of her mind, she asked her students to reflect on equitable participation through one of their assignments.

> My students do reflections, so I just asked them; I had some prompts about participation; what does it mean for equity in participation in class. And so many of them said, it was equality in amount of participation during class.

> So, then I thought, okay, we're saying this in the EQUIP session, and the students are also saying this, even though I wasn't sure. So, it convinced me more to do the equality thing.

Here Gwen shares that her students articulated the idea of equity as equality. This highlights tensions between Gwen's prior conceptions of equity, ideas shared in the learning community, and ideas that her students held. Gwen continued to reflect.

> And one thing I found with Leah, she's normally very quiet in class, but in her reflection, she talks about how she wants to participate, and sometimes she wants to jump out of her seat and say things, and I thought, "Really, I never thought she wants to participate," but she actually does, and I'm seeing now that she's always talking and she's always saying really deep things. So that's been fun to see her progress. I don't think I would've zoomed in on her if I hadn't read those participation reflections from them.

Gwen articulates this shift in Leah's participation (observed as 1, 4, and 4 contributions, during observations 1, 2, and 3 respectively). Of course, the equity metrics only tracked whole-class discussions, so the data can't speak to what happened in small groups, which were used extensively during Gwen's class sessions. Notably, Gwen realized that Leah's desire to participate wasn't evident in her actual lack of participation. This continued to problematize Gwen's initial model of equity that allowed "shy" students to remain quiet.

Last, Gwen shared her use of Kelly's check-in strategy and how that helped her better understand her students.

> I did "How is your semester going in terms of pizza and pizza toppings?" It was really eye-opening, and they were so creative. One person said, "I don't understand this prompt, but I'm doing fine." Some people said it is an extra-large pizza with so many toppings, it can't hold its shape anymore. You can kind of get a sense of how they are doing. Someone else wrote, "It was a burning-hot pizza that I put into my mouth too soon, and it burnt the roof of my mouth." It's cool because they can be creative and share how they are doing without actually having to share how they are doing. That was really fun. [. . .] From there it helped me say, okay, let's do a little break this week; I'm not going to give them a quiz, or not give them a reflection, to give them a break and help with that pizza issue.

The "pizza activity" allowed Gwen to learn more about her students' feelings without making them too publicly vulnerable. Solving the "pizza issue" allowed

Gwen to make changes to her instruction, holding off on the quiz and homework.

Observation four

This was the final lesson observed of Gwen's teaching. During this session, Gwen had an extended check-in with her students. Gwen shared that she felt the "energy level was very different" from other days, and Luca offered that there were "not many people in class" and that "break was coming up." Even though Gwen had worked throughout the semester to help students self-monitor, we see that the same dominant student continued to be the first to respond to the class when Gwen posed a question without explicitly monitoring participation.

After a handful of students shared how they were feeling overwhelmed, Gwen asked the class what they were looking forward to instead, and she went around the room asking each student to share something. Gwen gave individualized attention and responses to each student through this process.

GWEN: All right, can I hear, What is something you're really looking forward to over the break? Can we start with Lisa?

LISA: Um, just catching on like finals stuff.

GWEN: Catching up on schoolwork?

LISA: Like finals and doing stuff for my other classes.

GWEN: That's what you're doing during break?

LISA: Probably.

GWEN: Oh no, so sad. That's what you're most looking forward to for the break? How about you, Kriss?

KRISS: I dunno, my Mom's food.

GWEN: What are you having?

KRISS: Dressing, macaroni and cheese, yams, ham, but I don't really eat ham. [. . .]

LISA [*raises hand*]: I'd like to change my answer [*everyone laughs*]. I'm going to this Christmas place on Saturday; it's like a Hallmark movie. That's what I'm looking forward to. [. . .]

GWEN: Okay, cool. Thank you for resaying your answer. That sounds fun!

When Lisa offered that she would be doing schoolwork, Gwen responded with "That's sad," showing empathy and wanting something positive for Lisa to look forward to. After Kriss shared an idea, Lisa got excited, and Gwen came back to her, allowing Lisa to share something positive that she was looking forward to: seeing Christmas decorations.

After the extended check-in, class continued as typical. Gwen read some public comments on redistricting in California and encouraged students to leave comments. She also showed them a short video about gerrymandering and gave students more time to work in groups.

Learning community session four

The final learning community session was an opportunity for participants to wrap up the work that semester. Jerome provided data, and for the first time, women had more average contributions (2.54 average contributions) than men (2.33 average contributions). All racial groups had 2.5 average contributions. The reason for this shift was due largely to Gwen's use of an "everyone shares" strategy, where she individually checked in with each student.

Despite these changes in participation patterns, Gwen reflected how it was a "very hard class for" her, but it got "better after the check-in." It was clear that Gwen had grown to value her student check-ins and was using them regularly in her pedagogy. Kelly shared one more check-in strategy she liked to use.

> One [check-in] I got from a colleague of mine was "entrance song." I like to play music when the students come in. And the goofier I am, I think students appreciate that. [. . .] In different classes, if I got a sense of who was quiet in the room today, I would start the class with their entrance song, and ask the class to guess whose entrance song it was.

Beyond specific teaching strategies, Gwen continued to reflect on her understanding of equity. This time, she reflected upon an email exchange with me (the author) about a historical perspective on classroom participation, suggesting that to account for historical injustices, minoritized students should likely receive *more* than a proportional share of participation opportunities.

> I was thinking that if I use the strategy where everybody talks, I'm moving towards equality. So how do I push past equality and get *more* women to participate? Or more of other races?

Gwen continued the discussion of how to move past equality, which had been her goal in previous sessions. Given that she was teaching gerrymandering at that time, she discussed the idea of gerrymandering the student groups to promote equity.

> So, then I thought, what if I packed a group with all of the guys because only one person from each group participates—I thought maybe I can do that, because gerrymandering made me think of that.

In this case, if Gwen were to use the "packing" strategy for her particular classroom, it would mean only one man would share out during the group debrief rather than having debriefs that were often dominated by men. Gwen also wondered if it would make sense to use gendered check-in questions that might promote women to participate more. Kelly expressed caution at this idea.

> I would focus more on how to include counternarratives into the discussion. It's hard. I try not to group students based on identity because there are so many intersections. In all of my classes, I've had at least two students who identify as trans or queer, and being cognizant not to group them into a particular gender.

In Kelly's response, she notes complexities of gender beyond a binary notion and how gender stereotypes in the check-ins could have the opposite of the desired effect. She further connected this to a reparations view as follows:

> Moving from equality to reparations is something I'm still working through with my students. I try to look for questions about topics that specifically highlight or make space for specific counternarratives that are present in the room, more so than a question that might be stereotypical for a specific group. For instance, I have a student who is part of deaf culture in one of my classes, so finding ways to include in the class and discussions and their experiences, that has been a new thing for me this semester, to learn how to include this student and their experiences.

Here, Kelly acknowledged how a reparations idea of participation was still something she was considering and grappling with in her own teaching. This interaction highlights how the discussions could be mutually beneficial for participants and coaches alike. Gwen closed the meeting by remarking, "I wish we had two hours!" It was clear she found the meetings very useful both for camaraderie and for concrete strategies to implement.

SUMMARY AND REFLECTIONS

Gwen's equity learning community differed from Anne's in important ways. Kelly's coaching style as a counselor was very relational and focused on helping Gwen better flesh out certain dimensions of her teaching. These cases aren't designed to show the "ideal" community but to highlight how different decisions can lead to different effects. Kelly's focus on relationship building impacted how Gwen related to her students, even if she made fewer concrete changes to her teaching practice when compared to Anne.

From the outset of her participation, Gwen was using a variety of strategies suggested by mathematics education research. She actively engaged her students through group work, discussions, having students respond to each other's ideas, community building, and so forth. Despite using all these strategies, the racialized and gendered patterns of engagement in her classroom were largely inequitable. To address this issue, her goal was to shift the norms of her classroom and support students to better self-monitor their participation. She did this through three primary strategies: (1) making classroom norms explicit, (2) checking in with students, and (3) changing how she solicited participation after small-group activities.

Gwen spent a lot of time reminding students of classroom norms. She regularly paused within classroom discussions to check for understanding, explain the purpose of the discussions, remind students about norms such as "step up and step back," and explicitly ask for new voices. This was impressive given that college instructors typically introduce norms and then spend little time reinforcing them within class discussions, if they even have norming conversations at all. Despite regularly reminding students about norms focused on equity, it was still the most privileged students who chose to dominate conversations. I have observed this across many contexts: classrooms, faculty meetings, professional conferences, political debates, and even within equity learning communities. Supporting equitable patterns of participation requires explicit strategies and mechanisms to choose who participates.

With Kelly's support, Gwen developed new strategies for checking in with students. She began to use check-in prompts like the "pizza question" and used them to adjust her instruction. Gwen was already attuned to her students and building relationships with them, and Kelly's perspective as a counselor further amplified this.

The final adjustment Gwen made was to how she solicited participation after small-group activities. Before coaching, Gwen would solicit volunteers from each group, and the same few students would volunteer (the mixed-White men in the class). With Jerome's suggestion, she instead would randomly assign someone to share out before the group discussion (e.g., whoever had a birthday coming up next), to introduce randomization but avoid cold calling. Overall, this resulted in a wider set of students participating. This is a strategy Gwen continued to work with, and in her exit interview, a year after her participation ended, she described her continued use of the strategy as follows:

> One thing that I started to do with EQUIP was like getting students to talk in a group and then cycling through each person to be the representative. Okay. So, if I had four groups and three students in each group. I'd had student "one" share out everything from each group. Then, student "two" do it for each group, then student "three," and then I've covered everybody, right, and that's something that I learned in EQUIP that I've taken with me and kind of modified, and I think that's probably where probably the genesis of me then giving them—so if nobody speaks—giving them some time to talk and then doing a share-out type of thing.

The strategy of addressing silence with work time and then a share-out is similar to one of the strategies Anne used. However, in Gwen's case, the share-out was based more on randomization, whereas Anne picked specific students (generally women) with intentionality.

Like Anne, Gwen found the inequities in student participation to be jarring and eye-opening. These data served as a catalyst for change.

> The very first meeting [when] we had with the results, I thought, "I'm a mentor for women, and I support women, and non-cisgender males." Then I got my results, and it was totally disproportional to the demographics of the classroom, gender-wise. So, I thought, "Am I doing a service or am I doing a disservice? If students don't want to speak, should I just let that happen?" [. . .] I don't want to [cold-call students], but I do think it's important to have everyone participate.

As Gwen's statement shows, as a woman in mathematics, it was important for her to broaden participation beyond male dominance in the classroom, and she saw herself as a role model for women and nonbinary students. Gwen was also focused on racial equity, although she spoke more extensively about gender in the interview. This is consistent with our other experiences, that people more readily talk

FIGURE 3.1 Average contributions by gender in Gwen's class during the fall 2021 semester

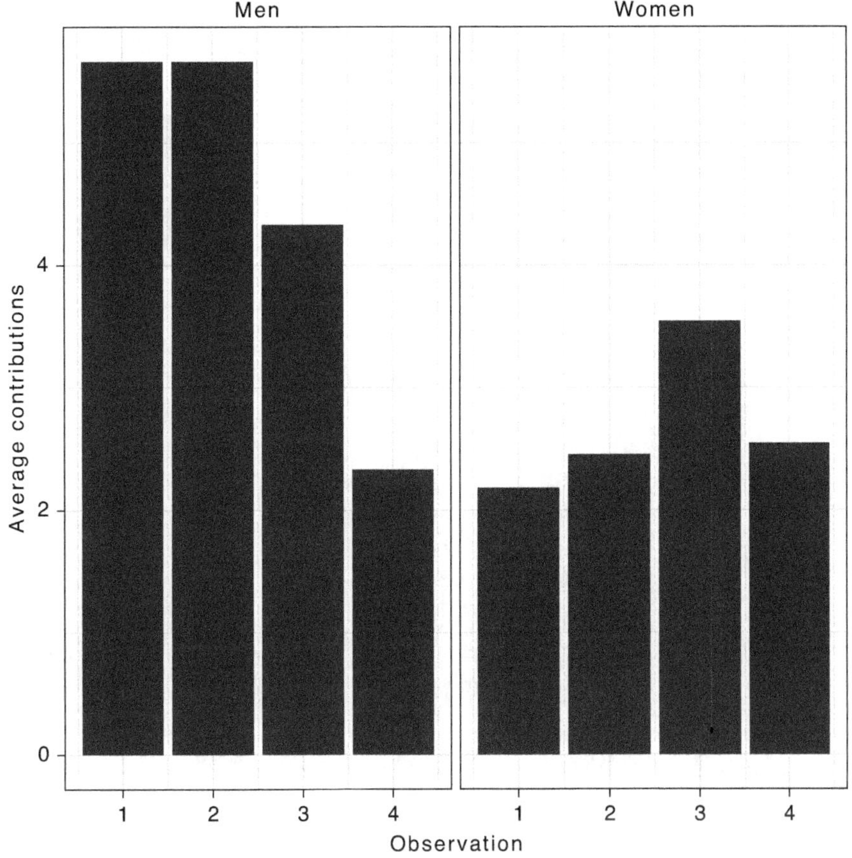

about gender inequity than racial inequity. The shift in gendered contributions is given in figure 3.1.

The results were slightly more complicated for racial equity, shown in figure 3.2. Overall, there was a reduction in talk from mixed-White students and a general pattern of increase for Latine students. For Black students, there was no conclusive trend. One explanation for the larger variation for Black students is that there were only two Black students in the class (in addition to one Black-White mixed-race student who is in the mixed-White category).

These shifts can be attributed to Gwen's additional attempts to build relationships with her students, make norms explicit, and better distribute group share-outs with randomly selected group representatives.

FIGURE 3.2 Average contributions by race/ethnicity in Gwen's class during the fall 2021 semester

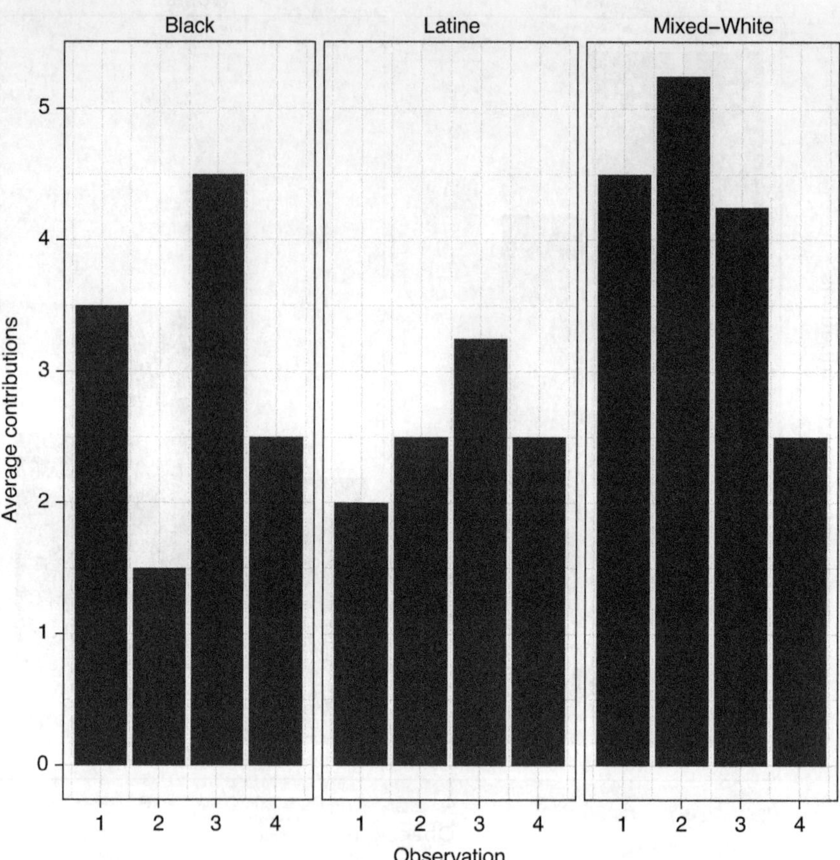

Gwen's story is instructive because she is a relatively experienced instructor who was already using many instructional strategies suggested by mathematics education. Simultaneously, without data and a supportive community, Gwen lacked intentionality in how she was creating participation opportunities. Thus, even though she was creating a variety of high-quality participation opportunities, those were taken up disproportionately by mixed-White students. Gwen reflected on how useful the community support was.

> I would look forward to every single [meeting]. In between, if I had things I wanted to discuss or needed advice on, I knew I had a group that would help me through it. I didn't feel alone. [. . .] It was such a comforting support to have because I felt like they could really give me great nonjudgmental feedback. I asked

> them some questions that weren't even technically class related, but they were just equity-related things, like why people write *folx*. [. . .] I always felt like an equal or a partner. [. . .] [Kelly] did a great job. I really liked interacting with her.

Gwen also highlighted how the data helped her track her progress. The data allowed her to see subtle patterns and changes she would not have noticed otherwise.

> It was much easier to see progress from a nonanecdotal perspective. Thinking about the first snapshot, seeing how I was so disproportionate gender-wise, and it didn't match my [prior perceptions]. And then seeing the data at the end. [. . .] So at least I felt like in the data I could see my progress, numbers-wise, not just "I feel like it worked," or "I feel good."

Here, Gwen highlights both how the data helped spur change and how they gave encouragement when she saw progress. In the years following her participation, Gwen continued to build on her experience in the equity learning community.

> [It] was like a snowball. It gave me techniques on how to [increase participation]. And then from there I started doing [new] things and then like doing more and other things.

Gwen followed up the snowball metaphor with a second metaphor of planting a seed. She described her intensive yearlong participation as valuable but not sustainable indefinitely. Yet this generative experience sparked her thinking and allowed her to continue her own growth independently.

> It's just like planting a seed. And then from there it has to be sustainable. Right? We can't keep going to these professional developments and keep having someone observe our classrooms. It's not sustainable; but to plant the seed and have it be up to us to be creative and take over and see. "Okay, how does that work for me in my classrooms and at my pace of growing?" [. . .] I think that's the power of EQUIP; it's just like you just keep thinking about it.

Through both metaphors—the snowball and the seed—Gwen discussed how the equity learning community empowered her to make ongoing changes independently. This is a trend that we have seen across learning communities. For coaches, it is useful to consider how to support growth in the moment as well as ongoing learning beyond formal support.

As she discussed in her intake interview, Gwen perceived a tension between bringing students into the conversation but not using cold calling, which she felt was "controlling and punitive." Before participating in the learning community, she simply avoided directly bringing students into the conversation because she didn't know how to do it in a supportive way. Following her year-long intensive engagement, she became more attuned to student body language.

> I look at student's faces now, and I will say, "Oh, it looks like you had a light bulb," or "It looks like you might have a question." A lot of times they do share. Now I'm just paying attention more to their faces and their body language and then reading it and then acting on it, whereas like that's not something I really did in the past.

Another strategy that Gwen started to use more frequently was to have "everyone share" some aspect of their thinking. This was a strategy she could use with reflection assignments, where there wasn't a specific correct answer and all students had a unique perspective. By setting the expectation that everybody will share, all students know that they are going to have a chance to share and can prepare before they offer an idea. Gwen shared the following over email:

> I notice my shifts, still—a semester later! In my math history class, I've also transitioned from asking students to voluntarily share their reactions to our reading and/or student presentations, to making EVERYONE share. It's been so much better! Sometimes conversations erupt, "That's what I wrote about in my reflection!" or "I thought the same thing!" Students also then start to share parts of themselves as related to the readings/presentations. EQUIP has had a lasting effect on my teaching. I went from a percentage of students talking in class to having 100% of my students talk! Same in my linear algebra class right now. It's become a norm. I love it.

Beyond her own self-perceptions, Gwen had an opportunity to be observed by the chair of her interdepartmental unit as a part of the promotion process. This experience provided further validation that the changes she made were positive ones.

> She was completely blown away by how everyone was participating. [. . .] She studies science education and biology education. She talked about how she noticed that I was dealing with their affect a lot, making sure they felt comfortable, and I asked to check in. She said she doesn't see it very often. [. . .] She noticed that I had a student present, and another student up front said, "Well, I didn't do that, and I may have done it totally wrong," and [the observer] said she felt

> like I had built a culture where being wrong was totally normal and the students felt comfortable saying they were wrong. She was really impressed by that. That relates to participation too. You get everyone to participate and say what they want—without judgment—and then they start to participate *more.*

Given all the changes that Gwen had made to her teaching practices, setting up the learning environment, and attending to student affect, she felt that there were noticeable differences in how she connected to her students.

> Now I feel like they come up to me after class. They ask me questions. And sometimes they'll break the boundary of just talking about content, right? And just ask me things outside of school. Even little things like saying goodbye when they leave the classroom. I feel like it's a nice thing. I don't know. It's such a small gesture. Or like they'll be like, "Oh, do you want me to help you erase the board," or "Can I put these chairs away," or you know. It's like it's just like we're a part of a community. And so those are the things I read that it's not like we're just here for math and then we leave; like, we are here for each other as humans and people. Those [changes] are the things that I think are kind of evidence for me that these things are working.

In addition to impressive changes in her teaching and student participation, Gwen made important notes of how her experience changed her thinking about equity.

> This idea of reparations I have been playing around with a lot in my mind. [. . .] Going through the program made me realize, like, let's get more voices into the classroom, but there's ways to do it. So, we're not embarrassing the students and they don't feel uncomfortable. So, I think that's my biggest takeaway. Get everybody to participate. Not just cold-calling on people but developing a system or the right environment over time so that people just want to participate. I think a lot about participation in class now, and before, I don't think I paid attention enough to it. Is everybody participating? I would just see if there was a lot of participation, like if people were speaking a lot; I still wasn't thinking about "Is everybody going to walk away from this, thinking that they participated?"

As Gwen describes here, her focus shifted from letting students be to recognizing the benefits of participation in a way that she intentionally supported students to engage in a way that they felt comfortable with. She continued that "These conversations about the reparational view have really changed how I view the classroom," but also that it was something she continued to grapple with and try to understand. She provided the example of students asking for an extension, and rather than telling them what they needed (i.e., simply providing a new deadline for the student), she would co-create an action plan with the student, asking questions like "What do you think is reasonable for you, considering your circumstances?" Overall, as all these statements show, Gwen's experience helped her think differently about her role and goals as a teacher, which was a catalyst that sparked instructional change.

KEY TAKEAWAYS

Gwen's case highlights a variety of features of equity learning communities and provides a contrast to Anne's story. Here, I return to two key takeaways for coaching work.

Equitable teaching intentionally supports specific students. As a mathematics educator, from the outset, Gwen's classroom looked much like what "best practices" in mathematics education would have suggested. She had interactive, inquiry-based lessons with students working in groups to explain their thinking. She explicitly set classroom norms, reinforced them with her students, and made attempts for students to build on one another's ideas. She even addressed issues of equity like critical race theory and gerrymandering directly in the course content. Yet this didn't necessarily lead to equity, as her initial data trends were very inequitable both in terms of race and gender. To make these "best practices" into equitable practices, Gwen needed to learn to use them intentionally to support specific minoritized students.

Gwen had some success using teaching strategies with this intentional focus. For example, she began to use check-ins to learn about individual students who might need more support. Nevertheless, many of the strategies Gwen adopted created participation opportunities for *all* students (e.g., preselecting students to share out from group time) rather than targeting specific students to share (with adequate support). While these did result in some reduction in inequities, the outcomes were not as drastic as in Anne's classroom, which used strategies specifically designed to elevate the status and contributions of women. This is one of the most important lessons in facilitating equity learning communities. Supporting instructors to create high-quality learning opportunities is not enough. Hierarchies are remarkably good at reproducing themselves, and as such, higher-status and privileged students (in this case, the mixed-White students) are likely to dominate the learning opportunities. To address this, instructors can explicitly support specific minoritized students to shift participation patterns.

Instructor perspectives and practices can shift together. Gwen's case illustrates how instructor perspectives can shift as they work through an equity learning community. For Gwen, these shifts focused primarily on what equity means. In her intake interview, Gwen expressed that equity for her included not putting shy students on the spot if they felt uncomfortable sharing. In the first community debrief, Kelly offered the idea that equity would relate to creating a classroom environment where *all* students felt comfortable to share. As she pondered this question, Gwen asked her students about it, and most students responded that in an ideal situation, participation would be equal. Near the end of the semester, Gwen started to shift toward a more historically oriented view of equity (i.e., reparations). She used concepts from gerrymandering—like cracking and packing—to think through how she might practically achieve this form of equity in her classroom. While Gwen did not feel as though she had fully aligned her perspectives with her teaching practices, this was something she continued to engage with even after her time in the learning community.

This case highlights the relationships between instructor goals, perspectives, and practices. If an instructor's goal is to support students to "feel comfortable," they are likely to produce very different participation patterns than focusing on "equal participation" for all students or even "reparations," in which historically marginalized students are afforded disproportionately *more* opportunities to participate and thus learn. For a coach, attending to these instructor beliefs and how they may shift over time with respect to data is an important leverage point in moving the work of a community forward.

Instructor perception and practice can shift together. Gwen's case illustrates how instructor perspectives can shift as they work through an equity learning community. [illegible] what equity means. In her [illegible] view, Gwen [illegible] that equity for her included not putting any students on the spot if they felt uncomfortable speaking in the whole community [illegible] equity would relate to creating a classroom environment where all students feel comfortable [illegible] this [illegible] her students about it, and most students responded [illegible] participation would be [illegible]. Near the end of the semester, Gwen [illegible] toward a more historically informed view of [illegible] from [illegible] and [illegible] did not [illegible] had [illegible] this was [illegible] engage with [illegible] in the learning community.

This [illegible] highlights the relationship between instructor perspectives and practices [illegible] they are [illegible] [illegible] [illegible] [illegible] [illegible]

CHAPTER 4

Elayne's and Sam's Stories: Learning Takes Time

A key element of equity learning communities is that change takes time. Research is clear that effective professional learning is ongoing and longitudinal, but still, short workshops are pervasive in higher education. Simultaneously, research highlights the difficulty of sustaining change. It's easy to promote change when there is an infusion of new resources, but when the resources go away, the changes often revert to the status quo as well. This chapter focuses on two instructors—Elayne and Sam—to provide two key takeaways related to learning over time.

Instructors develop responsibility for their students. Both Elayne and Sam entered their equity learning communities with the perspective that student participation was largely up to the students. They believed that students simply chose whether they wanted to be engaged during class. As Elayne and Sam revised their teaching and received data showing that these changes encouraged more students to participate, their perspectives began to shift. Elayne learned to reduce racial inequities through adopting new teaching strategies. Sam reduced gender inequities by using strategies like assigning competence, but racial and ethnic inequities remained, especially for Middle Eastern students. Reflecting on their experiences, both Elayne and Sam realized that they had much more power to shape participation patterns than they initially believed.

Change continues beyond participation in the equity learning community. Elayne's participation is described over two semesters and her exit interview was conducted two full years after her participation, which provides a window into her continued growth. Even after her participation in the community completed, she continued to revise her teaching to build a more culturally responsive curriculum. This echoes the experiences of other participants in this book, who continued to learn long after their engagement in their learning communities. Because exit interviews were conducted with participants at least a year after their participation finished, I can offer a more long-term view of change over time. In Anne's case, she continued to focus on participation even after her engagement with the learning community, such as by running workshops to share her learning with colleagues. In Gwen's case, she described the learning community as both a "seed" and a "snowball effect," which together spurred changes to her pedagogy and beliefs that continued to mature over time, even without further engagement with her coaching team or faculty peers.

ELAYNE'S STORY

Elayne participated in an equity learning community—with a coach and student coder but no other instructors—for two subsequent semesters of virtual teaching of a graduate-level public health course on behavioral science. Like in Gwen's case, Elayne's course content explicitly discussed racial disparities, but she was still learning how to produce racial equity in her class discussions. I provide a brief overview of Elayne's background, summarize the changes to her practice, and close with her reflections on the process.

Elayne was a White woman teaching public health at a public Hispanic Serving Institution. She was an assistant professor with about ten years of teaching experience, including graduate teaching assistant work. Elayne primarily taught master's level courses, which met once weekly for three hours. Teaching virtually over Zoom during the COVID-19 pandemic, she primarily used lecture and whole-class discussions, with some opportunities for Zoom breakouts. She described herself as "enthusiastic and interested in her content area but not always organized" because she sometimes jumped around between topics.

Elayne's initial conception of equity was that all students should have an "equal opportunity to succeed." Her approach was to provide additional supports to some groups to "level the playing field" (e.g., by referring emergent multilingual students to the writing center). In public health, Elayne taught courses about health

TABLE 4.1 Demographics in Elayne's class (fall 2020, via Zoom)

		Race/Ethnicity				
		Asian	Black	Latine	White	**Total**
Gender	Man	2	0	3	3	8
	Nonbinary	1	0	1	0	2
	Woman	5	1	6	7	19
	Total	8	1	10	10	29

TABLE 4.2 Demographics in Elayne's class (spring 2021, via Zoom)

		Race/Ethnicity				
		Asian	Black	Latine	White	**Total**
Gender	Man	0	1	4	4	9
	Woman	12	4	10	11	37
	Total	12	5	14	15	46

inequities, so discrimination, structural bias, and race were all topics that came up in the course material. Elayne joined the equity learning community with the goal to learn specific teaching practices to address inequities based on gender, race, or socioeconomic status because she did not currently know or use any.

Elayne noticed that even though her classes were mostly women, she felt that men tended to dominate class discussions. She also saw disparities between students based on socioeconomic status. Elayne was aware of her positionality as a White person teaching about racial disparities in health and recognized that the topics might cause her racially minoritized students to feel vulnerable or uncomfortable. The demographics of Elayne's class are given in tables 4.1 and 4.2.

Elayne's focus was on improving racial equity in class discussions. As it turned out, Elayne's baseline observation during fall 2020 was relatively balanced in terms of gender, so she decided to focus entirely on racial equity. Again, Elayne's first observation provided a baseline for understanding racialized participation dynamics. In this session, White and Asian students dominated the participation, with some participation from Latine students and no participation from the one Black student in the class. To address these issues, she implemented four primary strategies over the two semesters of her participation:

1. Flipping her class structure to begin with small-group activities rather than whole-class discussions. This ensured all students had a shared experience and more opportunities to contribute to the whole-class debrief.
2. Intentionally monitoring Zoom breakout-room discussions and checking in with students. Before her participation in the learning community, Elayne used breakout groups as an opportunity to catch up on her own work, missing valuable teaching and learning opportunities.
3. Using shared documents to organize group work. Rather than having students self-organize, as she did in the past, Elayne set up collaborative documents that all students could access. This allowed Elayne to monitor student progress, check in with groups that were stuck, and intentionally bring students' ideas from shared documents to the whole-class debrief.
4. Using effective facilitation strategies for whole-class discussions. Elayne began to use chat and "reactions" to get more students involved and would invite students to elaborate verbally, to elevate the status of their contributions. This helped Elayne move from *What*-level talk to more higher-level *Why* talk in her classroom.

Taken together, these strategies impacted racialized distributions of participation, as shown in figure 4.1. Elayne was able to elicit more participation overall and proportionally increased participation for both Black and Latine students.

The next semester, spring 2021, Elayne continued to refine her use of the above four strategies. She also began to use names more productively. She used student names to acknowledge contributions ("Thank you, Alex, for that idea") and to intentionally bring specific contributions into the conversation—for example, after a breakout discussion. This supported Elayne to build stronger personal relationships with her students. As in Gwen's case, Elayne noticed more students staying after class to talk with her, both generally and about the material. Elayne made records of when this happened and found students stayed after 75 percent of sessions, as compared to 0 percent before her participation in the equity learning community. Using all these strategies together, the distribution of participation by race remained relatively stable throughout the semester, as shown in figure 4.2.

As figure 4.2 suggests, the racial dynamics in Elayne's classroom had begun to shift, as Black and Latine students were participating similarly to, and sometimes more than, their White and Asian peers. Overall, Elayne described her

FIGURE 4.1 Average contributions by race/ethnicity in Elayne's class during the fall 2020 semester

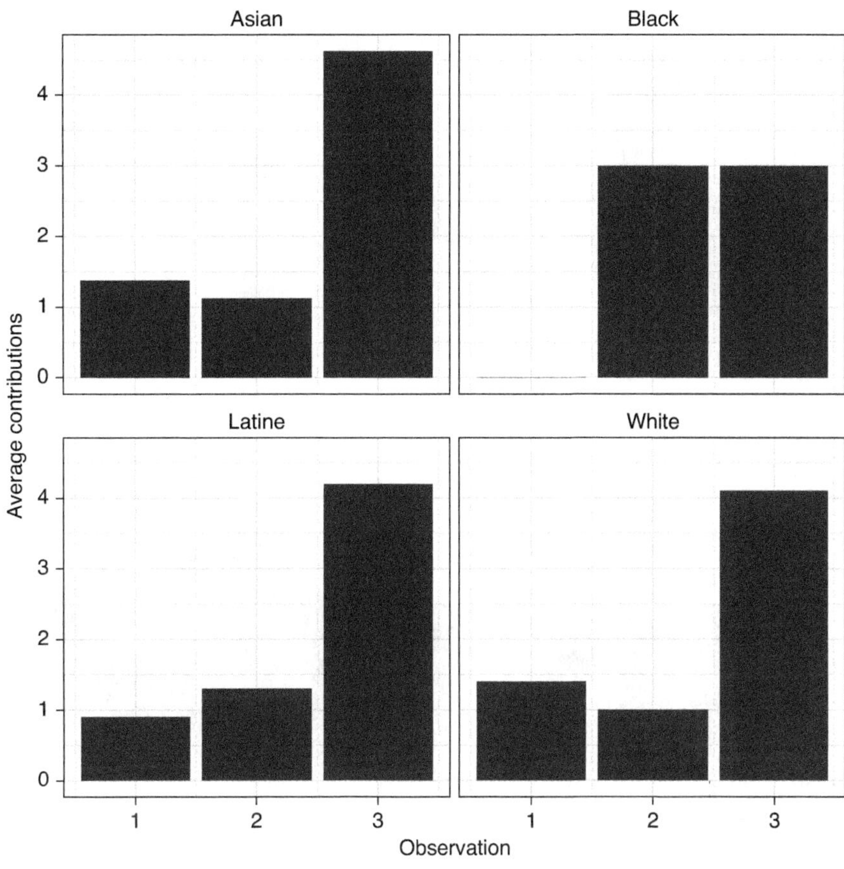

experience as shifting her instructional focus away from delivering content to designing an engaging learning environment.

> I'm seeing myself as being more responsible for being attuned to the experience of the students in the classroom and not just thinking that my sole responsibility is designing content that goes on the slide and thinking about what comes out of my mouth that clearly explains the concept. That's just half of the job, and the other half is making sure it's getting to them and that I'm giving them opportunities to play with and practice and internalize and ask questions and interact with the material.

Another new strategy that she started to implement after her time in the equity learning community was having students synthesize their ideas in writing.

FIGURE 4.2 Average contributions by race/ethnicity in Elayne's class during the spring 2021 semester

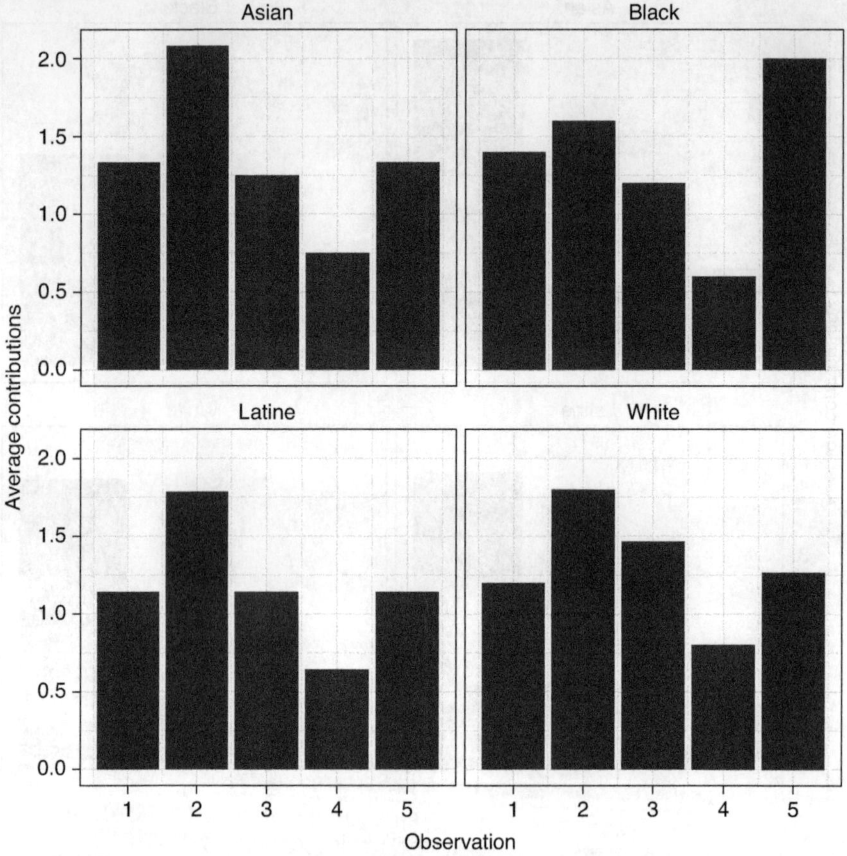

> I end each class with a group activity where they don't have to report verbally back to the class. I go back, and I visit each group individually and have one-on-one and small-group conversations. And then, later in writing, we'll distribute the responses. And so all those techniques combined give every student the opportunity to participate in a different way, which I didn't do before.

Related to shifts in her teaching approach, Elayne also began to see herself as having the ability to influence participation patterns in her class rather than attributing it solely to her students.

> Before, I had the mindset that, in any class, it's going to be the same five people participating. Through this opportunity I realized that this is not how it always has to be. You can do something about it. That was kind of like the aha for me.

Feeling empowered to change patterns of participation in her classroom, Elayne became better at noticing student behaviors even without the support of data. This connected to Gwen's ideas of "planting a seed" or the "snowball effect."

> The biggest thing that I'm trying to hold with me in my teaching is paying attention to who's participating. I'm thinking, "You know, it seems like, you know, people on this side of the room are participating more." I'm paying attention to "Is it only five people who are raising their hands, or am I only calling on the same five people?" Am I looking to the person who has previously raised their hand because I feel like they're going to participate again and get me out of that uncomfortable silence if we're in that situation? Now I'm noticing, not just presenting my planned activity and moving on, regardless of the participation. I'm stopping and taking those moments and just saying, like, "Hey, am I getting a high degree of participation?" If not, let's take a break. Let's try something different.

Elayne further remarked how certain participation structures (e.g., exclusive use of whole-class discussions) could reinforce her own racial biases, as she was the only one choosing who to call on, compared to more free-flowing interactions in small groups. Even though Elayne had more awareness of student participation and a slew of concrete strategies she could use, she still considered promoting equitable engagement as a "work in progress."

Given this view of work in progress, Elayne continued to experiment with her pedagogy for the two years between her participation and her exit interview. A key issue that she continued to grapple with was how her field often takes a deficit view of minoritized communities.

> I worry that the way that I present the material too often paints marginalized groups in not a positive way because we're talking about these health issues that they're experiencing. And I acknowledge like this is a result of systemic inequities. This is the result of racism, and we talk about why that is. But still, I worry that I'm not highlighting the assets of communities.

Given the emphasis on deficits within the field of public health, Elayne began to draw more heavily from a strengths-based approach. This allowed her to reframe conversations around public health disparities.

> Instead of saying "What are the factors that are putting this population at increased risk?" It's like, "What are the assets in this community that we could leverage to further empower these communities?" I encourage students to bring positive examples of their communities or communities that they care about into the lecture.

Elayne drew upon this reframing as a catalyst to support curricular redesign. Specifically, she started redesigning case studies to intentionally highlight student strengths.

> Everybody is coming into the classroom with different experiences in terms of ethnoracial background, gender identity, as well as socioeconomic status. When I'm designing the case studies [. . .] I'm thinking "Does this reflect a diversity of experiences?" Or "Is the way that I'm wording this question a positive way?" Or "Am I going to further a harmful stereotype?" Now I'm thinking more about it. I'm still learning more about how to do it.

This statement is powerful because it shows Elayne's continued reflection on her positionality as a White woman, the field of public health, and teaching about health inequities in a racially diverse classroom. Although she had made concrete progress with her curricular redesign, she was still able to acknowledge that it was a work in progress.

As Elayne began adopting a strengths-based approach, she noticed students were more open about their experiences with her, especially her students of color. This highlights how relationship building and the creation of spaces for authenticity, vulnerability, and trust can transform the teaching and learning process.

> I love that my students have started to be more and more honest with me, as the semesters have gone by, about [their] experiences.

Elayne remarked that her most recent semester of teaching (spring 2022) was "one of the most engaged classes" she had "ever had." Notably, it was a large class with fifty-five students, and she was able to translate the strategies developed from virtual teaching to in-person teaching.

Beyond the classroom, Elayne also started thinking about equity in her department meetings.

> In our faculty meetings and at our faculty retreat there's the same dynamics as in the classroom. I try to find ways to encourage individuals who haven't contributed in the large group to speak up and elevate the voices of the people who haven't been given the spotlight.

She summarized this as a process of "noticing" who is talking and who is not and "advocating" for others in a space to ensure that "their voices are heard."

SAM'S STORY

Sam's story provides another example of how learning takes place over time. Sam participated in equity learning communities for three semesters total while he was teaching in a synchronous online setting during the COVID-19 pandemic. Sam later served as a coach for a year, but Sam's coaching work is not included here due to space constraints. In Sam's story, I focus specifically on one instructional move that was instrumental to Sam's growth—assigning competence. (This was the same strategy that was so impactful in Anne's classroom.)

Sam was a White man teaching environmental engineering at a public Hispanic Serving Institution. He had been teaching for three years before he joined an equity learning community. Sam structured his class sessions with a mix of lecture and active student engagement; for example, through group design projects. Sam had a variety of international field experiences while living and working abroad, and he engaged in research in different locations around the world, which informed his multicultural perspective.

When discussing equity, Sam shared that "students start at different levels" and he "wants to get everyone to the same level in terms of outcomes." He mentioned that equity wasn't really something he thought about in his teaching until one semester before he joined a learning community. When he joined, he started "paying attention to quiet students" and wanted to understand "why they might not speak out" other than attributing it just to shyness. Sam was aware of masculine stereotypes in engineering, with men dominating class discussions and examples of discrimination in engineering firms. Sam described that he taught a lot of international students from the Middle East, and often they were ostracized in group work. He was trying to figure out how to better nurture cross-cultural support for these students.

In terms of teaching practices, Sam had attended a variety of offerings from the campus Center for Teaching and Learning. For example, he had his students do a values exercise that he learned from one of those programs, in which they wrote down three things they would look for in a teammate in their class, and had students use peer evaluations based on the criteria they generated. Nevertheless, most of what he learned wasn't concrete enough to shift patterns of inequity, which prompted him to seek further professional learning. The demographics in Sam's classes are given in tables 4.3, 4.4, and 4.5.

TABLE 4.3 Demographics in Sam's class (spring 2020, in person and via Zoom)

		Race/Ethnicity				
		Asian	Latine	Middle Eastern	White	**Total**
Gender	Man	2	2	0	7	11
	Woman	0	2	1	2	5
	Total	2	4	1	9	16

TABLE 4.4 Demographics in Sam's class (fall 2020, via Zoom)

		Race/Ethnicity				
		Asian	Latine	Middle Eastern	White	**Total**
Gender	Man	3	3	4	13	23
	Nonbinary	0	0	1	1	2
	Woman	3	3	1	7	14
	Total	6	6	6	21	39

TABLE 4.5 Demographics in Sam's class (spring 2021, via Zoom)

		Race/Ethnicity					
		Asian	Black	Latine	Middle Eastern	White	**Total**
Gender	Man	4	1	4	10	2	21
	Woman	1	0	2	5	4	12
	Total	5	1	6	15	6	33

Sam taught the same upper-division engineering design course for three consecutive semesters. Over that time, class observations were coded for thirteen lessons (spring 2020 = five; fall 2020 = five; spring 2021 = three). During spring 2020, due to the disruptions from the onset of the COVID-19 pandemic, Sam did not make appreciable changes to his instruction. However, he saw enough potential in the process that he decided to continue. Although he appreciated the interdisciplinary interactions within the spring 2020 cohort, he felt that the experience would be more useful working with other engineers.

During the fall 2020 and spring 2021 semesters, Sam recruited two more engineering professors from his department. In Sam's learning community, all three instructors would select a teaching practice to implement before the next meeting to allow a collective discussion about their experiences. Two of the main strategies the community focused on were the use of wait time and assigning competence. The easiest strategy for all three instructors to use was increasing wait time, which they all did almost immediately. I focus on assigning competence here because it was a more advanced instructional strategy.

Sam made durable changes to his instruction. He used private chat for one-on-one check-ins with students. Like Anne and Elayne, he shifted his questions away from *What* (getting the right answer) to *How* and *Why*, which included talking about processes and justifying solutions, respectively. He also used polls to check for student understanding and would even create a special Zoom breakout room to check in with students who were confused. Above and beyond all these changes, the most profound change was the use of assigning competence. He shared the following in his exit interview:

> The technique that I would say I tried to implement the most is talking to students before they would present in front of the class and priming them or giving them time to gather their thoughts.

During one of the learning community sessions, the coach suggested that the instructors could try assigning competence. The engineering team took this up with their own twist. Rather than selecting students to elevate during the flow of classroom instruction, they selected students *before* class began. When they were looking over student homework, they would preselect a few students who had strong solutions to the problem and who did not typically participate during class, and they would email them before class asking if they would be willing to share their work. For example, during the second debrief meeting during fall 2020, Sam shared the following reflection:

> I used assigning competence. [. . .] I opened the class with inviting two students at a time to share what they had expressed to me in an email about some problem that they encountered when doing their design and what they did to overcome it.

From the classroom recording, we can see how Sam used this strategy with his students. Sam opened the class session by inviting the two students to share their work.

SAM: All right, so let me enable the share screen, and Jake and Chloe are going to walk us through what their approach has been with the parcel data.

JAKE: Hi, my name is Jake, and the professor asked me to show you what I have so far for my project so far and how I found the duplicate data.

[*Jake continues to explain his approach about cleaning up the data and searching for errors in Excel. There is back-and-forth between Jake and multiple students who ask clarifying questions.*]

JAKE: Okay, that's all I have.

SAM: So, I have a question, I guess. One observation I had when we were emailing yesterday about this issue is that I really liked the way that Jake and his group used this kind of engineering judgment. Like, he looked at the total acreage that was calculated from the shape area, and it seemed too big, right, and then you went and utilized the tool in GIS Online to draw an area around the surface area and you found what was 474 acres or so. [. . .] So once you identified this duplicate issue and remove the duplicates. Did it fix the problem? Did you get a defined acreage that matched what you were measuring on ArcGIS?

JAKE: Well, I haven't done acreage for each of the zones, but I think I have most of the duplicates removed, and 474 is the total.

SAM: And that matches better with what you measured online?

JAKE: Yeah. [. . .]

SAM: This makes sense. [. . .] You'll see those gaps between parcels, but that's a good way to check, you know, Do the results that I'm getting, do they make sense? Of course, you're going to use those acreage values to calculate what the water demand is, and that's what's going to be used to design your entire system. So, I thought that this is a really good example of using engineering judgment and measuring something in two different ways to do a double check of your results to see if they make sense.

Overall, the conversation with Jake and the other students lasted about ten minutes, strongly highlighting his contribution to the class. Sam specifically noted his disciplinary contribution and assigned competence through describing Jake's good example of "engineering judgment" and checking the calculation in two ways. Next, Sam invited Chloe to share.

SAM: Chloe, would you be willing to share the approach that your group has been taking? [. . .]

CHLOE: The first thing that I did was I pulled in the nucleus zone. And then I just wrote the code over here. [. . .] For all of the residential parcels, I filtered those out and just looked at the bedrooms. An assumption I made was there was one person per bedroom, which I don't know if that's an okay assumption to make.

[*Chloe continues explaining the problem with back-and-forth from other students asking questions.*]

SAM: The really creative thing that I liked about her approach, her group's approach, is that they looked at number of bedrooms data for the residential uses. And they used that to get at what the design guidelines say, which is you need to use an assumption of gallons per person per day. So their approach is to estimate the number of people. [. . .] There could be multiple approaches that you use, and as long as you argue why your approach is complying with the guidelines and also accounting for future growth . . . then you'll get a favorable grade. There's no one approach that I'm going to require, but I would say that both the path that Jake's group is going down and also the path that Chloe's group is going down—and also some comments that Olivia just made—I would say all of those are really good approaches to rectifying this residential zoning situation.

This conversation also lasted about ten minutes, with Chloe having the spotlight, sharing her work with other students, and then Sam publicly acknowledging the strengths of her approach. Both examples of providing a positive spotlight to a student for an extended period provide strong evidence for assigning competence. In this case, all students were White, while Jake was a man and Chloe and Olivia were women. Thus, in this specific episode, the impact of Sam's strategy was more likely to help improve gender equity but not racial equity.

Sam also used the same strategy to bring in work from breakout groups. He would monitor student contributions during the breakouts, and when he identified women who were making strong contributions to the problems, he would draw attention to the quality of their work during the breakout discussion and invite the student to present back to the class. These invitations were often made privately (i.e., through private chat). Some students would decline, but if they did

FIGURE 4.3 Average contributions by gender in Sam's class over three semesters (fall 2020, spring 2021, fall 2021)

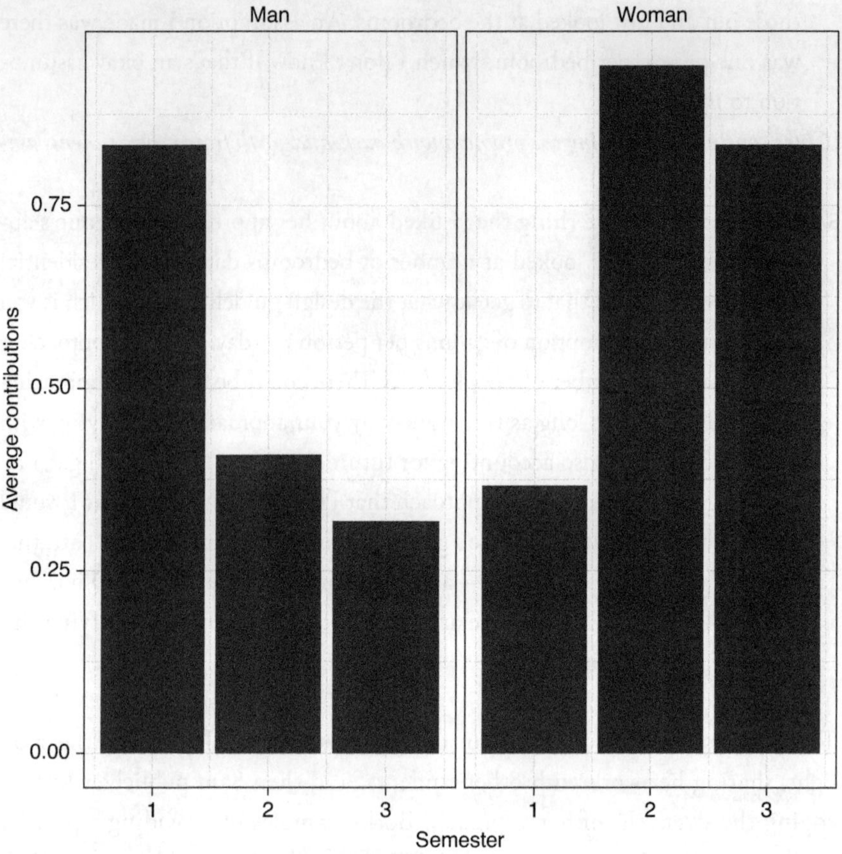

Note: During fall 2020 there were two nonbinary students in the class; there were none in spring 2020 or spring 2021, so I could not track longitudinal trends.

accept, he would call on the student during the whole-class discussion, and after she shared her correct solution, he would highlight the disciplinary contribution. Over time, Sam began to make progress in addressing gender inequities in his classroom. Figure 4.3 shows the average contributions by gender by class session, aggregated over each semester. Sam's data shows an overall trend, with women participating more in later semesters, and men participating less, semester over semester. Although this may appear inequitable from an equity as equality perspective, I would argue that given historical gender inequities in engineering, this is aligned with Sam's goal of supporting women in engineering.

In addition to addressing gender inequities, improving racial equity was also a goal for Sam. One of the key areas that Sam identified was a cultural divide and classroom-participation divide between domestic students and international students from the Middle East. The racialized patterns of participation are given in figure 4.4.

FIGURE 4.4 Average contributions by race/ethnicity in Sam's class over three semesters (fall 2020, spring 2021, fall 2021)

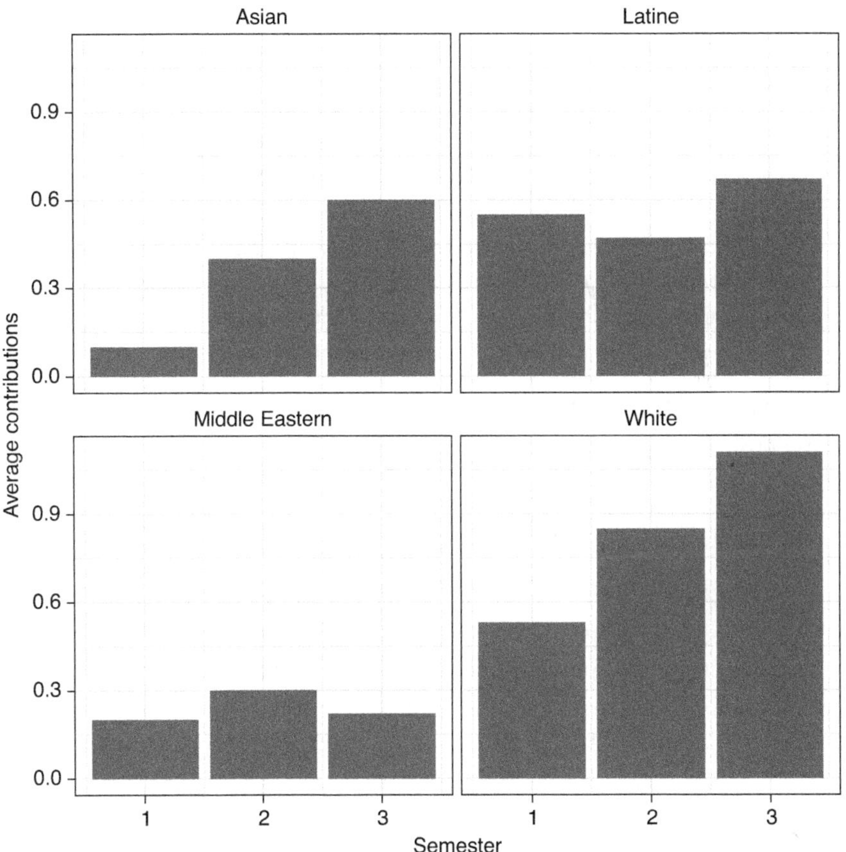

Note: During fall 2021 (semester three) there was a single Black student in the class, but because there were no Black students during semesters one or two, I could not track changes over time.

As figure 4.4 shows, although improving engagement with Middle Eastern students was a goal for Sam, he still had growth potential in this area. Overall, the data indicated that Sam was more successful in leveraging his new teaching techniques to support women in his classroom, but there is insufficient data to conclude why he was less successful with Middle Eastern students.

One of Sam's biggest takeaways was recognizing that he had the ability to shape participation patterns in his classroom.

> Coming into the project, I had no real concept that I could change participation in the classroom through little things that I do. It was something I had never really thought about before.

Although Sam made many changes to his practice, the one that stood out for him the most was the use of assigning competence. He came back to this topic repeatedly in his exit interview, offering powerful vignettes of his practice. The first involved a student named Marina.

> I remember clearly where it was a female minority student [Marina] that corrected a White male, more outspoken student in a breakout room, and this student, she rarely talked during the general session. The male student was pretty defiant about the fact that he was approaching it the correct way, and I saw the female student tactfully saying "No, you're not." I happened to be there observing, so I noticed that she was doing it the correct way and the other student was not.

As Sam noticed this situation, he was able to use assigning competence to elevate the contributions of the woman of color.

> I asked if she would explain to the class how she arrived at the problem, and so I thought that kind of opportunity was very positive.

As it turns out, this instance of assigning competence to Marina was the first time he ever interacted with her in his class. The following semester, Marina worked as a student researcher on one of Sam's projects and later became a student representative for the department. After graduating, Marina joined the graduate engineering program and received her master's degree. While all these changes cannot causally be attributed to Sam's use of assigning competence, it is plausible that his teaching did serve as a catalyst that helped Marina move from legitimate peripheral participation to being more centrally involved in the department. Sam was creating space for Marina's excellence to shine through.

Sam also discussed Sarah's case. Over four baseline recordings near the beginning of the semester, Sarah contributed only once. During Observation 2 (the fifth recording), Sam was trying a new strategy for the first time.[1] He had each student share their screen in turn to help facilitate the discussion. After viewing Sarah's plots, Sam made the following comments on the quality of her work:

SAM: All right, Sarah, your plots look really good, and I see you're starting on the pumping rate and the cumulative tank volume. So, I see that you put a standard pumping rate of two thousand. That's a really good number. How did you arrive at that number? This question is for Sarah.

SARAH: I looked at the hourly consumption, and I just kinda guessed at like a good average.

SAM: Awesome, yep, that's exactly what you wanna do.

Later in that same lesson, Sarah asked a question to Sam, which resulted in Sam asking everyone to revise their spreadsheets to incorporate Sarah's idea.

The next time we observed Sam's teaching, the impact on Sarah's participation was evident. Sam was publicly working through a problem in which wastewater from handwashing was being used to fill the tank to flush a toilet, as a water saving measure. In this episode, another student had suggested an incorrect solution, which Sam mistakenly took as correct. However, during the discussion, Sarah had the confidence to correct the mistake he made in his computation.

ADAM: So, we would just subtract that 6.9 from the 8.2?

SAM: There you go, so you can imagine that this system is still hooked up to the potable water. So if it doesn't get enough drainage water from the handwashing station it will supplement that with potable water, so 8.2 minus 6.9 you get that response, multiply that by 5, that's how much water savings this device right here would cause, would result in, for each household of five people.

SARAH: Why would you subtract it? Wouldn't the saved water be just the 6.9 times 5, because toilet flushing is the bigger number?

SAM: You'd be saving water from what usually fills up the tank back here. So usually potable water is used to fill up this tank. Right, on average that's 8.2 gallons per person per day. So instead of using 8.2 gallons of potable water to fill up this tank, you're using . . . 6.9 of those gallons are coming from the sink.

SARAH: Right, so if you're asking how much water would be saved, wouldn't it be 6.9 times 5, because if you subtract it, that's how much water you still need of potable water, right?

SAM: Oh yeah, you are, you're right. [. . .] Thank you for correcting me. [. . .] Awesome, Sarah, I'm gonna give you a thousand extra-credit points. Because I do want you to correct me when you see me say something wrong. You know, I'm a person, and I make mistakes sometimes and miscalculate things sometimes.

Here, we see Sarah asks a question to clarify one of Sam's computations. Sam initially brushes off her response with a quick explanation, yet Sarah persists in asking again, explaining to Sam where the error was. This exchange was so memorable for Sam, he recalled it during his exit interview.

> [Sarah] started speaking up more during class discussions and offering solutions to problems. During one class, a week or two after I had used [the assigning-competence] strategy with her, I was going over a solution for the class, and she interrupted me to let me know that I had made a mistake. Naturally, I felt a bit embarrassed about my mistake, but inside I was also so proud that she felt confident enough to interrupt me in front of the rest of the class!

Sam's progress was notable. In a field that was traditionally dominated by men, he had created space for women to publicly share their brilliance. Simultaneously, Sam recognized that there was still work to be done to better engage his Middle Eastern students, and this was an area of future work for him.

KEY TAKEAWAYS

Instructors develop responsibility for their students. Both Elayne and Sam shared in their exit interviews how their perspectives on student participation had shifted. Initially, they both believed that participation was mostly up to the students and that vocal students would participate while shy students would not. However, after working through an equity learning community, developing new strategies, and seeing data show that their actions could impact student participation patterns, both Elayne and Sam realized that they had control over who participated or not. This was a key insight that allowed them to continue to grow beyond their intensive engagement in the equity learning community. As a coach, it is important to build instructors' self-efficacy so that they can see their own responsibility and capacity for redressing classroom inequities.

Change continues beyond participation in the equity learning community. Elayne's story showcases how changes continue over time and can be far reaching. After her yearlong community participation, she continued to experiment with new ideas and began to redesign her curriculum to be more culturally responsive and build on student assets. Although this was not part of her coaching experience, having support and data for a year gave her a sense of her own self-efficacy and allowed her to continue improving. This is like Gwen's statement that the learning community "planted a seed" for her to continue learning. Similarly, Elayne noticed inequities in faculty meetings that she was previously less attuned to. From this, coaches can take away the importance of building a foundation so that instructors can continue to learn. Equity learning communities can be an asset for lifelong learning. Coaches can amplify this to find opportunities to further engage past participants, by recruiting them as coaches, hosting social events, or otherwise having them share their learning with new participants.

CHAPTER 5

Brian's and Kelly's Stories: Moving from Participant to Coach

This chapter provides a deep dive into the coaching process. It focuses on two former equity learning community participants—Brian and Kelly—who were later recruited as coaches. These two cases are not intended as perfect examples of coaching. Rather, they are concrete examples of how former participants can effectively coach their peers even if they don't have formal training in educational coaching. Here, I highlight two key takeaways from the chapter.

Relationships provide the foundation for change. A key theme of this chapter is looking at how Brian and Kelly fostered relationships with their instructors and how they leveraged these relationships to have difficult conversations about equity. Although this chapter focuses mostly on relationship building, one key purpose of relationship building is to support instructors in adopting new instructional strategies. Comparing Brian's community and Kelly's community, there were more concrete strategies shared in Brian's community, which resulted in Anne adopting new teaching strategies, while Gwen's experience focused on developing new perspectives. Much of this came down to the student assistants. Marie was much more direct in sharing specific research-based strategies, while Jerome shared fewer strategies. Fortunately, over years of this work, I have developed a treasure trove of effective strategies and written a book as a resource for future coaches.[1]

Experiences as a participant support coaching. A second key theme is how Brian and Kelly used their prior experiences as participants to connect with their instructors. For example, Brian often reflected on his own challenges as a participant with teaching equitably to foster connection. Prior experiences also provided a concrete model for what coaching could look like.

Additionally, to support participants to serve as coaches, we built a coaching learning community in parallel to the equity learning community. This community consisted of me, Sam (from the prior chapter), Brian, and Kelly. This space supported regular check-ins and building strategies for coaching. The community met roughly once per month, between the debrief meetings with the individual equity learning communities.

BRIAN'S STORY

This section focuses on Brian, who was the coach that facilitated Anne's equity learning community (which had another faculty member named Ramesh). Brian was a previous participant in an equity learning community in fall 2018. Brian drew upon his prior equity learning community–participant experiences to build a trusting learning environment. I provide a brief set of reflections from Brian from his time as an equity learning community participant, which helps contextualize his coaching practices.

Brian was a Black man and a mathematician by training, with interests in mathematics education, especially in advancing racially minoritized populations in math. He had been teaching for over a decade with a commitment to social justice and had participated in a variety of professional-development projects, contributing to mathematics education from his positionality as a Black mathematician. Brian was committed to lifelong learning and improvement. He was teaching mathematics at a public Hispanic Serving Institution.

Brian's early reflections on participating in an equity learning community help provide insight into his coaching strategies. Brian emphasized the value of data.

> Having data about what is happening is way more useful than I ever imagined. Because without it, you can tell whatever story you want, right, about what happened in the classroom. You can focus on whatever part of that day or whatever student interactions were so positive that you want to take away, and that can be your whole premise for measuring your effectiveness when it comes to equity issues in the classroom.

He reflected it could be "frustrating at times" to work on instructional change when there were already so many things to do. Although it was challenging, he also felt it was necessary.

> Thinking about equity and actually doing the hard work to make changes within yourself and want to actually improve equitable outcomes, they're just two different things. But this helps me put my finger on that a little bit more. Like we can talk about equity all day, but it's a different level to reevaluate your own practice and step down from that pedestal that as faculty members we like to sit on and realize that there might be not just some things you could be doing different, but there's a lot of room for growth for everyone, no matter where you are in your practice.

Overall, Brian believed his participation helped him translate his equity goals into practice. Brian's openness and reflectiveness, combined with his deep experience as an instructor and an advocate for equity, all played into making him a very effective coach that helped support Anne to make impressive changes to her teaching. Here, I provide concrete vignettes to illustrate Brian's coaching style. Each of the vignettes shows how Brian built relationships to support his community through difficult conversations.

Vignette one: It's personal

This episode took place during the first debrief meeting in the fall 2021semester. After checking in with participants about their general impressions on how things were going, Brian and Marie (his student assistant) provided Anne with data about gender inequities in her classroom. Marie shared that 70 percent of contributions came from men, even though men were only about 55 percent of the class. After sharing these data, Brian interjected with the following:

> If I can add something, I think that the data from both of your classes are really representative [. . .] especially coming from two faculty members that are expert teachers but who haven't had a chance to look at the data. [. . .] [You are] beyond the average instructor who's coming into EQUIP that hasn't thought a lot about trying to address these kinds of issues. I think it shows that a lot of these things you're being thoughtful about, and so I just wanted to mention that.

Here we see the dynamic between Marie and Brian as they supported participants. Marie brought in the data, and Brian encouraged the participants even when they had difficult data (i.e., data showing that men were dominating). In response to Brian's words, Anne said, "This is great; it's exactly why I wanted to do this." The way Brian contextualized the numbers helped build a sense of common purpose rather than judge and evaluate the participants.

Later, when the community was discussing Ramesh's participation data, some of the negative trends found in the data could be easily seen as threatening (e.g., lower-level *What* talk and only a smaller proportion of students participating). This was especially true because this was a semipublic community space in which Ramesh might feel the need to save face with more-senior colleagues.

After providing some difficult feedback, Brian discussed his own experiences receiving challenging data. Brian made himself vulnerable, and this created the space for trust and instructional improvement for Ramesh. Had Brian not had prior experiences as an equity learning community participant himself, it could have been more difficult to soften the impact of the feedback and build trust.

> Some of the things that I noticed when looking at the data and comparing my notes with Marie's were, with student talk, White students seemed to dominate, and maybe that was a little bit consistent with the demographics in the classroom, of course, as well. Most of the contributions that you solicited as a teacher were more *What* and *How* questions as opposed to *Why* questions. There seemed to be balance between the shorter responses and the medium-range responses, which was interesting to notice. [. . .] The main things that stood out to us that you could focus on is fostering more participation from the folks who didn't participate in that first video session. And thinking about how to solicit deeper-level questions. And asking for *Why* when students have responses. And thinking about, you know, how to also elicit sort of more thoughtful responses, as opposed to the short responses. One thing I remember, you know, as I was going through the [equity learning community] process myself was my own evolution of what participation would look like and what that meant, and so. Like at some point my goal was to get everybody to participate once, you know [*laughs*]. And I got really close to that, and they were all like one-word responses [*continues laughing*]. And I'm like, well, Is this how I want to measure equity in my classroom? And so I think a lot of these things are kind of personal about how we want to see things play out and what we can do with the data.

In the final segment of this episode, Brian describes how as a *participant* he aimed to get all his students to talk at least once. When he felt accomplished in doing this, he then realized that they were only one-word responses, so they were surface level and not as meaningful as he had hoped. In this discussion, Brian was laughing most of the time when he was discussing his own struggles as a former participant. This allowed him to relate to and validate Ramesh's experiences. This trust allowed Brian to have difficult conversations in ways that could support Ramesh's further growth. Brian framed equitable teaching as a difficult endeavor, normalizing the struggles his participants faced by discussing his own experiences.

Vignette two: It's weird and awkward

The second vignette took place during the second debrief meeting in the fall semester. During this episode, Anne shared with her colleagues that she wanted to talk to her students about the importance of equitable classroom participation but that she was afraid it would be "weird and awkward." After Anne brought this issue up, Brian validated her feelings and shared a resource, a mathematics-education blog post from Stan Yoshinobu, who directs the Academy of Inquiry Based Learning, which focused on the importance of getting student buy-in for active learning.[2] Brian shared his own stories of math trauma as a student in calculus class. This created space for Anne to share her frustrations about gender inequities and other social-marker-based inequities. Brian labeled this as "math trauma," which was a profound concept for Anne and one she returned to in her debrief interview, as explained in Anne's chapter.

ANNE: What do you guys think about talking about why participation is valuable or having [students] read something or talk to each other about it? [. . .] Have you ever tried that? Is it weird? Does it just make it more awkward later? [. . .]

BRIAN: I think it can be valuable. [*Shares about Stan Yoshinobu's blog post.*] I know a lot of people have been terrorized about talking in math classes. As you describe, Anne, I have this story, this memory of being called to the board in calculus class in high school. I can remember the problem: Here's a function, graph its derivative, and I was clueless, and I just stood there; you know, it was just the worst experience. And I have a colleague who has said, for years, like, "I can't force my students to do group work because it terrifies me to have to talk to people in my class." And so, these are all real. [. . .]

ANNE: It really bothers me that it's so delineated down gender lines and down, you know, other kinds of lines. [. . .]

BRIAN: I think it's, it's what, it's what they call math trauma. [We need to] have a space in the classroom for some healing of that, I guess. Like, if nobody else is going to do it, you know. And so maybe we can—we're like the last chance, in some sense, before they leave the math classroom forever.

At the beginning of this vignette, we see how Anne first made herself vulnerable in asking for help about something she worried could be "awkward." Brian was responsive to the concerns, by sharing resources and a personal story that also made himself vulnerable. This led to a longer conversation around math trauma and connected to the importance of their work as the "last chance" to "heal" that trauma for students. These were all ideas that resonated with Anne and profoundly changed her perspective. This was only possible because Brian and Marie had created that safe space that allowed for these types of conversations.

Vignette three: Small-group racism

The third vignette took place during the third debrief in the spring semester (the second semester of participation for Anne and Ramesh). During this semester, Ramesh was focused on small-group interactions. Although he followed a single group for most of the semester, as the semester went by, he did record some of the other groups, which allowed for more diversity in the conversations. In this third vignette, the community looked at a video clip of small-group interactions in Ramesh's classroom, in which a group of four women was working together, but not working together particularly well. Even when Ramesh walked over to get them engaged, there was some struggle to get the students to work together. In this debrief, Brian brought up the idea that other students could be ignoring the Black woman in the group. Brian kept the conversation open with his positive attitude and a bit of humor, but still suggested how to make that student visible and highlight her competence.

BRIAN: I thought that you said all the right things, Ramesh, that you should be checking in with each other, and you kinda leaned in and asked them to support each other a little bit and reminded them of that.

RAMESH: Yeah, any advice from the three of you? I can get them to turn around, but I don't know what else to do.

BRIAN: One of the things I was thinking, so there's one student, it looks like maybe she's a Black woman, and I wonder how that is playing out in this dynamic. There's no way to know, but that's a thought. What's going on with her, and why isn't anyone talking to her? I could say the same thing about the woman to her left. But I wonder who is struggling the most, and it's hard to tell.

RAMESH: Yeah, so Laura, the Black woman in the front left, she is the best student out of these four, the one diagonal from her is the next, and the other two are in the low C range, like borderline passing.

BRIAN: That's interesting, like the students might not know all of that. So I'm wondering, Why aren't they turning to Laura for help [*laughing*]? Those are some things that came to mind for me.

RAMESH: They did check answers with each other as I prodded them, and like Marie said, that was their interaction. So they were at least checking answers, but I have to imagine that they didn't all get the same thing every time, so what did they do then?

ANNE: It looks like Laura is trying to interact. Like she borrowed the notebook, and then she had to tap her [the other student] on the shoulder, like "Hey!" whereas the other woman with her iPad is totally not even looking up, even when you came over.

BRIAN: There might be some opportunities to assign competence; you know . . . I'm trying to think of a situation where you could direct them to check with someone else in their group about their solutions. If you have a feeling—this might not be the case—that Laura might have something to offer the others in the group, there might be changes for you to say, [. . .] "Hey, I really like Laura's approach" or "Did you guys see what Laura did over here?"

Here, we see how Brian brought up how race could be in play during this small-group interaction. Again, Brian is seen laughing to lighten the mood as he brings up a difficult topic. To help generalize the situation for Ramesh, Brian shared the assigning-competence strategy. This helped frame Ramesh's issue within a broader set of issues rather than pinning it solely on Ramesh and his teaching.

Ultimately, this focal group was only observed once during the spring semester, so there wasn't an opportunity to follow up on the group with further empirical data. In his post-interview, Ramesh directly called out this moment and the further conversation it led to as impactful.

> I also recorded a couple of other groups the last few weeks to see what the differences were. [. . .] [There was a] discussion about what our ideal group work would look like. There was so much that I got even from just watching those videos, even not being coded. Um, just about like how groups run in the class. [. . .] That was really eye-opening.

Here, the "other groups" that Ramesh is calling out were related to the specific episode described above. The transcript above illustrates how trust and vulnerability can be valuable in interactions that attend to equity at the core. It's also notable that Anne was a part of this conversation and that all the participants were comfortable engaging with these difficult issues together.

KELLY'S STORY

The second coaching case focuses on Kelly, the coach who facilitated Gwen's equity learning community (with another instructor Jorge). Kelly was a prior equity learning community participant for a year. I provide a brief background of Kelly and her experiences as a participant, to contextualize her coaching work. I partially attribute Kelly's effectiveness as a coach to her ability to draw on her experiences as a counselor and counselor educator. Overall, her approach differed from Brian's group, focusing more on student relationships and less on concrete intervention strategies. This section focuses on how Kelly used her past experiences to foster a productive learning community.

Kelly was a biracial woman (Black-White) teaching counseling at a public Hispanic Serving Institution. She had been teaching for two years since graduating with her PhD and spending a few years as a graduate teaching assistant. Kelly taught counseling students who were part of a cohort-based program. Kelly described her teaching ideology as grounded in constructivist, Vygotskian, and liberation-psychology practices. She felt that equity is often oversimplified; for example, like the picture of three children of different heights standing on boxes. She saw equity as understanding, acknowledging, and valuing what students know so she could build on it. In contrast to Brian—who had more formal leadership roles in his community—Kelly was relatively early in her career, but she did have a wide range of pedagogical and counseling expertise.

One shift that Kelly made because of her participation was to use more Zoom breakout rooms and collaborative shared documents. This created more opportunities for students to work together and for Kelly to check in with specific students. She then purposefully called on specific students after breakout sessions.

> It was a really big takeaway to me to take a step back and let them engage in small-group discussions and different activities. It doesn't always need to be content, content, content, content.

After spending a year in an equity learning community, Kelly described a variety of new insights that she had developed. The first was realizing that certain racial groups were dominating her class discussions.

> One of the things we were noticing was a handful, I think two or three, White students who identified as female. [. . .] When we looked at the data, we saw that there was a lot of participation from specifically the White female students.

Kelly contrasted the high levels of participation from these three White students with the rest of her class, which was "mostly Hispanic and Latine." As an educator committed to racial equity and social justice, this became an obvious point of intervention for her as she shifted her teaching practices. Once Kelly recognized that this pattern was happening in her classroom, it gave her the space to try new strategies to shift the conversational dynamics.

> [I] have a lot of White female students, who in terms of population are a minority in the class, but they are taking the most talk time in the class. [Initially,] I was using a lot of "What" questions, but the students with minoritized identities weren't participating at the same length or space. [. . .] So, I started to utilize "How" and "Why" questions to follow up and help them dive deeper and exercise more space and autonomy within the class.

By providing variation in the types of questions she asked, Kelly shifted the goal of the discussion away from reaching "the answer" to gaining a better understanding of students' processes and reasoning. This opened space for more rough-draft thinking and different strategies and representations rather than focusing only on the one most efficient method of obtaining the correct answer. In addition to probing with deeper questions, another insight for Kelly was to release control back to her students.

> I know it sounds pretty basic, but one of the key takeaways, right, for me is relinquishing control. You know, it's funny, because in counseling we always say let the client lead. And we think that that translates into our teaching practice and modalities. But what I found with my practice was that I was really reluctant to

> have students break up into small groups. [. . .] Instead, I did the old-school whole-group lecture, which I was justifying, saying it was a group process and group dynamics, which is actually kinda against what we do in counseling.

Kelly noted how there was a tension between best practices for providing counseling to a client and the types of pedagogical strategies that were typically used in counseling. This was an interesting realization for Kelly as she began to practice what she preached, breaking up her class into small groups and supporting greater student autonomy. This is consistent with the observations my team has made across hundreds of classrooms, in which extensive use of the whole-class discussion space creates an environment that prevents many students from meaningfully participating unless there is explicit intervention.

At the time of her final interview (a year and a half after she was a participant), Kelly reflected on how she was continuing to have new insights and how the process helped her find greater joy in her teaching.

> I'm teaching a curriculum class. Students have been working on consultation teams. I might offer ten slides and tell them this is what we're doing, and they spend the rest of the time doing it. I can go around and ask them questions and see how they are doing. That's been really enjoyable. So, a class that I didn't really like [when I taught it previously] turned out to be one that I'm enjoying.

As Kelly describes here, the curriculum class is one that she would typically teach through lecture and whole-class discussions, but having opportunities to give students an interesting task, break them out into small groups, and then intentionally check in with the students was more enjoyable and more effective for her.

Vignette one: Setting the stage

In the very first learning community meeting, Kelly spent a lot of time on introductions and allowing every member of the community to share their goals and aspirations for the process. She asked both participants to introduce themselves and talk about what brought them to the meeting and what questions they were trying to answer. Jorge was wondering how to increase participation in his classroom while balancing external pressure from departmental evaluations to cover content. Gwen shared that she was thinking about what equity really means in the classroom and how to best facilitate it. After hearing from participants, Kelly was very upfront in sharing where she was coming from, which helped set the tone for her community.

> I always find it helpful to share a little bit about how I approach mentoring and facilitating this type of discussion group. This is my first time facilitating this specific type of group mentoring with fellow colleagues, so it's a little intimidating. I love theory, so there are definitely things I take into account when I think of overall curriculum, shaping classroom dynamics, and what that can look like. For content, in terms of some of the pieces related to mathematics, it might be more sharing between the two of you in terms of strategies. I'm just here to help in terms of facilitating the conversation and providing some insights. It's more of a shared dialogue than me coming in as the expert and saying to you "This is how you should do that." I'm definitely limited in my own scope of practice, but I do have some of my own perspectives and experiences in teaching my counseling students that I will bring in to help you both. So I have your questions, and I think both of your questions will be guiding questions for us throughout this process, and we can't answer those in a few sentences. It's going to depend on what's happening in your classroom, and Jorge, you mentioned evaluations and what's happening at the department level. I think we'll probably integrate those two questions into our work together and add more as we go through it too. At this point, I think we can turn it over to Jerome to share with us. Last year when I experienced this, I would come into the meeting, and Daniel would check in, see how we're doing, and then we'd move into looking over the data and reviewing the data. [. . .] And if there's specific things you want to review, let me know, because you're the driver of this meeting.

Kelly's statement here did important relational work because she made clear to the participants how she would be facilitating the meetings and was setting a stage to empower them to take the lead to meet their own goals.

Vignette two: Everyone shares

As a coach, Kelly was very intentional in how she structured opportunities for the instructors to share their experiences and making sure she was understanding what they shared. For example, during the second debrief, Kelly began by sharing a structure for the meeting.

> In starting up today, let's do an initial check-in, and then we'll get right into the data and then wrap up with some questions or goals for next session, to kind of check in during our next session in November. So checking in, I'd love to hear one thing that's going well and then one thing that's still kind of so-so.

After this invitation, both Gwen and Jorge responded with how things were going. Gwen noted that she was feeling low energy in her class.

> In the beginning of the semester, I felt like students talked so much more. [. . .] My students seem to have no reaction to anything I say, so I'm having a hard time. The good thing is [. . .] this group of students is the most conscientious group of freshmen I've ever had.

Kelly responded as follows:

> So the plus being the conscientious, the kind of in between being not really knowing where they are at. Feeling that they are slowing down a bit but not really knowing why.

Later, Jorge shared his feelings, and Kelly revoiced in a similar way. Kelly then invited the student researcher Jerome to share, and finally, she herself shared how she was feeling. When she did so, she connected what Gwen shared to her own experiences.

> So, Gwen, when you mentioned that your students are slowing down a little bit in terms of energy, we're noticing that in one of our cohorts. We actually did a midterm survey to get a sense of where they are at, and many of them are expressing fatigue in moving from online to some of their classes being in person. So at the moment, we're trying to figure out ways to support them during this time, because some of them are feeling stuck, unmotivated, or uninspired. Other than that, I guess things are going well.

Kelly's strategy of having everyone in the learning community share in the same way was a powerful way to build relationships and level the playing field in terms of power structures. In sharing how she was doing, she connected to what Gwen had earlier shared, validated that struggle, and offered a concrete idea (surveying the students) in terms of what her program was doing. There is a lot of important relational work that took place during a very simple and structured exchange. In future debrief sessions, Kelly used a similar structure to open the conversations.

Vignette three: Elevating student ideas

This vignette begins after Jerome had shared some data with Jorge about levels of participation in his classroom and discussed the depth of student contributions (*Why* versus *How* versus *What* contributions). As a follow-up, Jorge shared some struggles he was having with getting students to participate in his class and how he felt that students were more willing to share anonymously.

JORGE: One reason I don't use the chat, and instead started using Kahoot! [a course-response system], is because Kahoot! is anonymous, and I feel that students are more likely to share their response if they feel like they won't be judged. Even if they don't know, I just tell them to submit something. [. . .] Here's where I get the conflict. Should I base the questioning on those who are responding only, or how do I increase the participation from those who haven't responded, who tend to be more shy? I can use Kahoot!, but if you don't see the names, it's hard to find out who contributed.

KELLY: If you're using Jamboard or Google Slides for your activities, one thing Daniel told me—because I hesitated to cold-call people when moving to a whole group from breakout rooms—a strategy he shared was when you're bouncing around the breakout rooms [. . .] I would listen in on the conversation and say, "That's a really good idea; when we get back to whole group I'm going to call on one of you to share." What I do a lot right now is say, "I need two volunteers. If I can't get two volunteers, I'm going to call two folks to share what their group talked about." So sometimes I'll frame it like that, so it's not singled in on one specific student but in terms of the group. "So how did your group work through this process," or "What is one question your group has," or "What was one barrier your group faced when trying to solve this math problem?" Framing it as a group rather than an individual sometimes helps with prompting folks to share too. Where they don't have to say, "I struggle with this," they can say, "My group talked about this," or "This was a struggle," or something that worked well.

JORGE: With Google Slides, I could also use the coloring system.

GWEN: I like how you adapted the Google Slides; I think that was really creative. One other thing that I also do, like Kelly was saying, going around and listening to the groups. When I hear someone who says an idea, and this is someone who usually does not participate in class, I say something like "Ooh, I really like that idea. When we get back to whole group, would you feel comfortable sharing that with everybody?" They usually say yes. Sometimes they say, "No I don't want to," and it's okay. I let someone else share it. But I think that helps to get those voices.

Here, we see an example where Kelly drew upon her prior experiences as a participant and connected them to her current teaching practices.

Kelly served as the coach in a learning community where all other participants were mathematicians, but she was a counselor. This meant that she was not familiar with the disciplinary content that was being discussed. Simultaneously, this meant that Kelly had unique skills, given her background, that were less typical for mathematicians to develop. Kelly reflected on these affordances and constraints as follows:

> At first, I was intimidated when you asked me to coach, especially in mathematics education. How do I transfer what I do as a counselor educator to coaching math educators? [. . .] The team aspect was essential. Jerome, having a math background, was able to provide specific strategies, and he knew the language and the concepts. [. . .] I thoroughly enjoyed it. I found that there were a lot of ways that what I do translates into what I think you were hoping for in the consultation piece and support for these educators.

One of the main reasons that Kelly found the consultations to be very productive is because the mathematics faculty wanted to become more adept at working on relationships and supporting students at a personal level, and that was Kelly's area of expertise.

> I looked at the data and listened to them and heard what they were wanting. The two [participants] we were working with were working on the interpersonal part. They felt "I have the strategies and logic, but I'm not getting the feelings." And for me, I get the feelings but needed to learn the strategies.

REFLECTIONS ON COACHING

Here, I provide reflections on coaching from both Brian and Kelly. I characterize their reflections according to the core features of an equity learning community: (1) Empirical data create local urgency; (2) learning communities collaboratively process the data; and (3) instructors make iterative, incremental changes to practice.

Empirical data create local urgency

Brian elaborated on how data helped organize his coaching work. He likened the first time that participants see data to an "aha moment," which creates a sense of urgency to change.

> I think the first time they see the data is a big surprise. Maybe not a surprise, but it's an aha moment. [. . .] If they make some changes and go back and see the changes in the data, that can be an aha too. I think that helps with "buy-in" to the process.

In addition to creating that "buy-in" to the process, Brian used the data as the basis for conversations around concrete changes.

> The data provoked conversation and gave things to bring in that we could try from week to week. It also gave opportunity to bring in tools that instructors could start thinking about to decide which ones to make a part of their practice and add to their tool belt. And the data gave evidence that the tools could have an impact on what was happening in the classroom and how students are participating.

Despite the positive aspects of the data, Brian still felt that "data has limitations" but was useful for provoking conversation. He further wondered what could happen if all "instructors had access to this data on a regular basis." Brian talked about this extensively, how he wished he could always have data on his own classroom. He laughed and remarked how he wanted someone to keep coaching him.

> I need to do this again. I'm like "When am I doing it again?" Somebody coach me, please. I would do it every semester if I could!

A final purpose of the data that supported Brian in his coaching was to get a more objective view on the classroom. As he reflected on his role as an instructor, Brian recognized that instructor impressions were biased and often based on a single positive interaction, rather than realistic reflection of what instructors experienced.

> Without the data, you would just be stuck with what the instructors said happened [*laughs*]. The instructor's perception is subject to a lot of bias.

Although the data provide a more objective view, Brian also recognized that the data could be frustrating for participants at times.

> It takes a special kind of person to be able to take critical feedback and use it to grow. I think it's normal for frustration. [. . .] [This involves] dealing with the emotions that come from looking at that kind of feedback. [It may not] match your perceptions and [. . .] you may personally not feel like you have a bias. [. . .] [But] if the data is consistently reflecting something, then you have to face some questions about yourself.

Kelly also found value in using data to drive the work. Simultaneously, she recognized that there can be resistance to using quantitative data for equity, so she appreciated the nuance in how data were used as tools to support the process, but not to speak for themselves.

> When it comes to equity and diversity work, currently—even in myself—there is resistance to numbers. And there are reasons for that. In many ways, people use numbers as a way of avoiding policy change or structural change, by just having representation. [. . .] What I appreciated about it was the process. The actual process was not *just* looking at participation data; that was a tool. Even within the tool, coding with teacher solicitation and talk length provided more descriptive data than just how many students raised their hands or how many students participated. So, it was much more dynamic. It was helpful because I appreciate nuance.

Kelly further highlighted the role of data in providing a foundation for learning, reflection, and change because the data helped her move beyond an abstract and theoretical vision of equity to the specific and concrete. She analogized this to when she has students do case presentations in her classes related to their counseling work.

> I think about when I do case presentations with students. If they come in and just talk about their case [without data], we can still dive in and provide feedback. But seeing the tape, that provides me with "at that moment, and that time, you said this, and if you said this instead, it would've been more encouraging and engaging." Seeing the data was helpful. Jerome was awesome about giving a summary because then I could just look at it.

Kelly further described how she and Jerome hoped to have participants share five-minute video clips of teaching to enhance the depth of data, but it was something that they never managed to implement in this current iteration.

Learning communities collaboratively process the data

The collaborative nature of equity learning communities requires relationship building. Given the possible emotional challenges that come along with doing authentic equity work, Brian spent a lot of effort in getting to know the participants, building positive relationships, and creating community support. Brian talked about how he would check in casually with the participants each meeting.

> Checking in with them at the beginning of the meeting and just to ask them how it's going is nice. People find that helpful because we don't really ask that to each other all the time.

Brian contrasted the check-ins with typical meetings, which often get down to business with little relational work up front. Interviews with Anne and Ramesh made it clear that this approach had a positive impact. For example, Anne likened the meetings to getting coffee with friends.

> I liked how [the meetings] just started with checking in. It was kinda like we were getting together for coffee. The time was taken to do that, so I got to know Ramesh a bit, he had a baby. I learned other stuff about him. Brian I knew already, so that was different. But it was really nice to see him regularly.

Brian likened himself to a DJ. His role was to make everything come together. Marie, his student assistant, provided the coding and data. The coaching community provided resources and concrete suggestions for instructional change.

> My role was like a disc jockey. Marie would point out things that she saw in the data, and I could go [to the coaching community] for ideas on how to support the instructors with those things. That process from meeting to meeting was the most helpful.

Brian's description here highlights how equity learning communities function as a part of a larger system. In this case, the combination of student input, instructor perspectives, and the coaching community all worked together to set him up for success. Even though there were formal roles within the learning community, it felt very fluid for participants. As Anne remarked,

> It was very comfortable. I thought everybody had ideas and shared them and felt good doing that. [. . .] I felt it was very collaborative. There were these roles like "I'm the coach," but those roles weren't very obvious when we were talking. I'm not sure how you engineered that, but it worked really well.

Anne's comment points to how natural the community space was, even though it was intentionally designed to foster certain types of learning. The mutual support between Anne and Ramesh was something that Brian fostered through community building.

> Anne and Ramesh were giving so much support to each other. There was a lot of cross communication. Like a triangle.

Finally, even though Brian's role was that of a coach, he still valued being exposed to new instructional strategies.

> The things that I'm taking in during the coaching role, I'm definitely thinking about how to use those for my own teaching.

As Brian's comments highlight, equity learning communities have the potential to produce a variety of forms of learning for actors at multiple levels (i.e., student researchers, participants, coaches).

Like Brian, Kelly focused on how to build community between participants, as was evident in the vignettes above where she has all members engage in the same forms of structured share-outs.

> It's egalitarian, right. I'm not coming in and saying how to do things. I ask, "What do you need?" and figure out if I'm the right person to help or if we need to get some other resources to support what you want for your students.

This egalitarian approach was connected to her view of learning as a community process, not as simply the coach providing knowledge to the participants. Within the community, she felt that "there was a lot of shared learning, back and forth. [There was] relationality." This shared learning underscores the collaborative element of an equity learning community.

Although learning is collaborative, different community members may be in different places with their practice of equitable teaching. For example, while Gwen had formal training in mathematics education, the other instructor—Jorge—was in a relatively traditional environment that constrained his ability to implement new teaching strategies. This required Kelly to develop strategies to transition between participants and ensure everyone was benefiting and that participants were able to give feedback to one another. Kelly described the following:

> We had a pair of faculty members who were at different developmental levels. To me it seemed that we found ways of gently transitioning between the two, so they both felt heard and like they had space. [. . .] Communication between cofacilitators with that was really helpful. And what we want to see with groups is that they are giving feedback to each other.

One way that Kelly set up these gentle transitions was through the affordances of the virtual-coaching medium, which allowed her to privately communicate with her cofacilitator.

> Zoom was helpful for the consultations because the cofacilitator and I could message each other. In coaching, you can often do silent signaling with someone you're well acquainted with, but it takes a while to get to know each other's physical cues.

Like Brian, Kelly reflected on the importance of learning collaboratively in the coaching community with Brian and Sam.

> I think, as a community, there was a supportive and positive group dynamic. It was growth fostering and mutually empathetic. [. . .] The fact that we were from different disciplines, and even generations, I think that was pivotal for fostering the community that we fostered. There wasn't a competitive nature of trying to prove that I'm a better coach or that I know more.

Instructors make iterative, incremental changes to practice

Brian also discussed how data supported instructors to iteratively improve their practice. As they began to make changes, the data gave them evidence of impact and helped them continue to take up new strategies, as an iterative cycle of improvement.

> The data changed over time to provide evidence of impact. I definitely saw them picking up the strategies we talked about and finding their own ways to implement them and bring their own strategies to the mix.

Brian saw this form of iterative instructional improvement at the classroom level as something that could be embedded into a larger campus-wide systemic change effort.

> This is something really concrete that faculty, departments, learning centers can do if you're interested in increasing outcomes for all students. Having something to point to is helpful.

From his view, there was a need for changes at many levels of the system, but one of the most important sites for change was teaching practices.

> When it comes to actually impacting students, it has to happen in the classroom. We have to unpack what's happening in the classroom. That's where students are spending their time. That's basically where they get one-on-one with individual instructors. And if instructors are only thinking about the content, then they are not serving the students. I feel like these kinds of professional development are so important, and they can be instructional. Focusing on equitable instruction through this project is where I've found the most bang for my buck.

As Brian continued to talk about the approach, he discussed how he felt it "could have a national impact."

Kelly highlighted how the coaching process was not designed to overhaul teaching practices overnight but, rather, to build on participant strengths to support smaller ongoing improvements.

> With coaching, it's not that it's supposed to be awe-inspiring or so profound that you changed my world. With coaching, you're starting with what they already know; you're starting with strengths they already have. [. . .] It's developmental, it's education-based. We want to work with what you have. We want to help develop your agency, autonomy, skills, and abilities.

Kelly continued, sharing the role that the data played in support of those incremental improvements. She also articulated the goal that hopefully growth would continue even after the consultations were completed.

> [The] consultations really pulled in the educator's goals, capacities, and skill set. How do we use that from a strengths-based approach, and how do we use that with the tool, looking at the metrics, to create a more holistic picture? And hopefully have those skills and capacities continue in future classes in how they approach the work and how they talk about the work.

Kelly also described some of the forms of ongoing learning that the participants were engaging in and would hopefully continue to engage with.

> It should be those little things. For Jorge: "I feel more comfortable trying some new strategies, even if I'm still feeling the pressure of evaluation." For Gwen, [. . .] she had questions around equity, and it was helping to answer her questions, but it also led to more questions.

Finally, for herself, Kelly reflected on how serving as a coach fostered her own ongoing learning.

> Especially because I did this the year after I was a participant, it reinforced the things that I learned as a participant. Now I'm facilitating and teaching others about the same skills and what worked for me and what didn't. [. . .] Doing it with peers was new, and that was empowering as an assistant professor to coach someone whose status was above mine, hierarchically. [. . .] That was empowering for me.

Given the joy and value that Kelly derived from the process, she further reflected on how she could implement similar learning cycles in her own research.

> This process has definitely resonated with me; it's definitely stuck with me, and now I'm thinking about ways to use it in my own research. There's a model I'm thinking about now with K–12 educators. I could work with someone in literacy education, and my role might be thinking about how this contributes to helping with toxic stress for teachers. How does this go beyond strategies for inclusiveness and equity and actually also be a model for the interpersonal support and community support and the empowerment of the educator. How can we study that a bit more and dive into that? [. . .] Professional development often doesn't stick, and I think one of the reasons is that there's no community behind it; there's no investment beyond the two days. So how do you create something that is more of an investment and also with that reciprocity so that everyone is learning and it can also be sustainable?

As Kelly's statement shows, participation was impactful and had many applications well beyond the confines of classroom teaching.

KEY TAKEAWAYS

Relationships provide the foundation for change. The six coaching vignettes in this chapter highlight the intentionality with which the coaches built relationships with their participants. Equity data can easily feel scary or judgmental, so coaches need to create a space in which participants can safely process through the data. Brian often softened the conversation by using humor and connecting the discussion to his own experiences. Kelly drew on her relational strengths as a counselor. Both coaches created a sense of "in-it-togetherness" to allow collective improvement, rather than allowing the instructors to feel lost in their own struggles. The takeaway for other coaches is clear. Strong relationships need to be fostered between the coaches and participants for this to work.

Experience participating in an equity learning community supports coaching. Relationships are the foundation for change, and having relatable experiences is one effective way to build relationships. Both Brian and Kelly drew on their own experiences as equity learning community participants to relate to the instructors they were coaching. Brian was especially effective at sharing his own challenges to help his instructors feel better about their own struggles. Had Brian and Kelly not previously received data on their own teaching, it would have lessened their credibility and made it harder for them to connect with their instructors. Prior experiences as a participant also provide a model of coaching for new coaches, giving them access to concrete teaching and coaching strategies. A lesson for future coaches is to spend time going through the same types of learning that you want for your participants.

CHAPTER 6

Bringing It All Together

In this chapter, I bring together key ideas from across the previous cases, vignettes, and reflections. This chapter begins with a summary of learning for the six focal instructors who participated in equity learning communities. This provides an opportunity to compare, contrast, and synthesize the six learning trajectories described above. The next section focuses on the process of participants becoming coaches and how to build coaching cohorts. The final section focuses on how to scale up this approach on a campus to create sustainable professional learning for equity.

PARTICIPANT LEARNING

This book provides an in-depth look at the engagement of six instructors who participated in equity learning communities. For each instructor, I emphasized different facets of the learning process. For Anne and Gwen, I illustrated the iterative nature of learning connected to data, through cycles of reflection during a single semester. This shows how instructors iteratively refine their practice between debrief sessions and how the accumulated changes to practice have a growing impact on equitable student participation. For Elayne and Sam, I focused on the longitudinal aspects of the learning process and how their learning sustained and continued to deepen over time. For Brian and Kelly, I focused briefly on their learning as participants to provide the context necessary to understand how their own participant learning later translated into their work as coaches. Of course, while each of the six cases includes a variety of these elements,

I intentionally focused on different parts of the learning process for different instructors to provide the reader with a more holistic picture.

The participants profiled in this book were diverse along a variety of relevant dimensions: race, gender, disability, discipline, teaching experience, professional experience, and so forth. As one would expect, the learning process for each participant looked different. There was no single end goal that all participants were expected to reach. After all, the equity metrics are customizable, and equity learning communities are designed to support the individual needs of each educator. Not surprisingly, each participant-instructor had their own trajectory, area of focus, teaching strategies, and key insights. Although instructors made improvements, there was still room for continued growth. For example, Elayne remarked that she was still refining her use of strategies, and Sam recognized that he still needed more work to reach his Middle Eastern students. Despite individual nuances, there were some crosscutting themes and overall improvements across instructors that were impressive. I summarize those here.

Across the board, instructors were surprised when they first got their data. As Brian described, it was an eye-opening "aha!" moment for instructors. These six cases are consistent with our broader work across dozens of instructors. Although instructors may intend to include every learner in discussions and believe that most students participate in discussions, these intentions and perspectives rarely match the data. Fundamentally, the data provided the catalyst for change.

Another consistent feature across the instructors is that they initially believed that the patterns of participation in their classes said more about the students than the learning environment and that instructors saw student participation as mostly out of their control. As instructors began to implement new strategies and saw corresponding shifts in the distribution of participation, they realized that they had more control over student participation than they had originally thought. Both Elayne and Sam acknowledged this explicitly in their interviews. Similarly, Gwen shifted away from allowing "comfortable" students to participate to supporting all of them. Anne addressed this in terms of prior math trauma and trying to make students feel comfortable participating in her class regardless of their prior experiences. Overall, this is quite an empowering finding. Whereas faculty initially didn't see it as their responsibility to get all students meaningfully participating, their participation in the equity learning communities gave them concrete strategies and a renewed sense of responsibility for engaging their students. And, moreover, their involvement in the community provided them with knowledge and tools to support the students who were most marginalized in their classes, as a step forward toward remedying historical injustices.

Overall, the instructors profiled here were attempting to include their students in classroom discussions even before they joined their learning communities. However, for the most part, instructors had few explicit strategies that they could use to address inequities as they arose. In this way, it was evident that the instructors were exposed to **equity talk** about making an inclusive space but had less in terms of concrete strategies and practical skills to make that happen in their classrooms. This was even the case for instructors like Brian and Anne, who had over a decade of experience teaching and organizing for equity in mathematics education. Their time in equity learning communities changed that. All instructors who participated made a variety of changes to their teaching, and more impressively, their time in the program served as a catalyst that promoted ongoing learning even after the coaching was completed.

Changes to instruction

One set of strategies that participants used with great success was whole-class discussion strategies. These included having students raise their hands, practicing wait time, and having multiple hands go up before calling on someone (not just calling on the first student to raise their hand). In cases where students didn't volunteer, a quick turn-and-talk (or think-pair-share) could break up the class, improve processing time, and allow for intentionality in who the instructor called on. By talking with students during the partner discussion (or small-group work), instructors set up their students to be successful during the whole-class debrief. These forms of assigning competence were particularly powerful, as Anne's and Sam's cases highlighted.

While all these strategies are useful in general, they become powerful tools for promoting equity when the instructor is equipped with data on student participation, because knowledge of the disparities in participation with social-marker specificity helps educators set targeted goals and plan actionable next steps. Recognizing that most instructors may have biased perceptions of who is participating, and how they are participating, in their classrooms, the data become a key catalyst for change. By explicitly using teaching strategies to increase the quantity and quality of contributions from students who, according to equity metrics, initially had a lower status, instructors were able to improve participation from minoritized students. Anne's classroom provided a strong example of fostering a community where women felt that they belonged and their contributions were valued, thus encouraging them to participate. Sam's assigning of competence to a previously quiet woman in his class resulted in her becoming so comfortable that later she corrected a mistake he made during a lecture. Not only did these episodes have a huge impact on the students in the classroom, but they also left a lasting impact on the faculty participants, cementing their understanding of the value of equity metrics paired with community support and specific equitable teaching strategies.

Another set of strategies focused on small-group work. Initially, many of the instructors relied heavily (almost exclusively) on whole-class discussions, except for Gwen. In their reflections, both Kelly and Elayne remarked on how moving between small-group breakouts and whole-class discussions promoted participation by providing students with time and space to reflect on the prompts individually and with their peers. Similarly, Anne used turn-and-talk as well as partner-work time to break up her otherwise interactive lectures. Even Gwen, who initially used a lot of group work in her class, learned key strategies for selecting and sequencing student contributions from small groups. Rather than simply having the loudest students from the groups share out, she began to use strategies like preselecting students to share. Other instructors (like Anne, Sam, Brian, and Elayne) would check in with their students during work time to elicit ideas and to find productive ideas from lower-status, marginalized students and explicitly bring those students into the whole-class discussion in a positive way.

Another area of focus for participants was the *type* of questions that they used. The hierarchy of *Why-How-What* was made explicit in the coding scheme, and as a result, faculty participants aimed to improve the depth of questioning they used to engage more students in higher-level reasoning. Across the board, faculty participants generated deeper awareness of the types of questions that they wanted to ask their students.

Another type of change focused on the activities that instructors themselves used. For example, Anne developed some very creative ways to get students to move around and interact with different students using ideas of rows and columns and proofs from linear algebra. This type of deep connection between the disciplinary content and equitable teaching strategies is laudable. Others, like Elayne, began to design their case studies and student discussions with more intentionality so that they could build on student-community strengths rather than deficits.

Finally, there were a variety of other smaller changes that certain instructors made that were unique to their practice. For example, Sam learned how to better use student names. Gwen began frequently checking in with her students. Elayne started talking more with her students as they volunteered to stay after class. All these strategies rehumanized the educators' instruction as they got to know and invite students to bring their whole selves into the classroom.

Changes in student participation

Each faculty member had their own goals, so the changes in participation looked different across classrooms. Anne was teaching in a mostly racially homogeneous environment, so her key area of focus was gender. Surprisingly, even though Anne was a strong advocate for women in mathematics, this would not have been evident from the initial observation of her classroom teaching, in which men dominated the discussion. Yet, over the semester, the impressive changes Anne made to her instruction resulted in significant shifts in the quantity and quality of participation by women in her class. Initially, men would quickly shout out answers to Anne's prompts, but by the end of the semester, a significant cohort of women began to take on leadership roles and provided the backbone to key disciplinary conversations.

Gwen was focused on both gender and race in her classroom. These two social markers were tightly interconnected in her participation data because the few men in the class were mixed-White students. More interestingly, Gwen discussed her desire for both gender and racial equity in her classroom, and this was evident from her classroom activities that focused on a variety of topics around racism, such as partisan and racialized gerrymandering, critical race theory, and "driving while Black." Yet, in the learning community sessions, much more of the conversation focused on improving gender equity. This is consistent with our other experiences, where in general, for folks in the US, it tends to be much easier to talk about gender than race (notably, all members of Gwen's learning community were people of color—Asian, Black, Latine, and biracial). There is a true complexity to talking about racial equity openly in learning spaces in the US, where we have found it often doesn't come up unless explicitly prompted by a facilitator. Nonetheless, the net impact of Gwen's efforts improved both racial and gender equity in her class. Sam's case also showed how it is often easier to make progress on gender equity than racial equity.

Sam was focused on racial and gender equity in his engineering classes. This was mostly to support women and international students from the Middle East who tended to be marginalized. Overall, Sam made significant progress in improving gender equity in his class. This didn't happen in the first semester he participated, but it was evident in the later semesters, due to his priming and assigning-competence strategies. At the same time, Sam made less progress in improving participation for the Middle Eastern international students. This remains an area of continued growth for his teaching and equity efforts.

The other three instructors focused only on race (and not gender), given their classroom demographics and disciplinary context. For example, Elayne taught public health, and most of her students were women; their participation was well-represented in her class. Even though she taught about racialized health disparities, she was still figuring out how to do this as a White woman teaching mostly students of color. The strategies Elayne adopted did have an impact on her student participation; she learned to engage many more of the Black and Latine students in her class, and this sustained across semesters. After her participation in the learning community, Elayne delved deeper into racial equity, by drawing on students' community and cultural assets in lesson planning and execution, which undoubtedly resulted in more empowering experiences for her students.

Both Brian and Kelly were also focused on racial inequities, although their data stories are not shared here in-depth. Briefly, Brian made some progress in redressing racial inequities, by increasing participation from Middle Eastern and North African students in his classroom, but still had low levels of participation from three Filipino students. Overall, Kelly was able to make progress in increasing the levels of participation by students of color relative to the White students. This was especially true for Latine students and one Filipino student, who had the highest levels of average contributions throughout the semester (but not during the first two sessions). Nonetheless, addressing racial inequities is complicated and requires ongoing work each semester.

Changes in instructor perspectives

All these impressive changes to instruction and student participation were connected to—both supportive of and supported by—instructor changes in perspectives.

As described above, the insights that instructors had about the importance of participation in the learning process and their own impact on student participation was paramount to the change process. Beyond this, instructors had their own unique insights, based on the composition of their respective learning communities.

For Anne, the idea of prior math trauma was something that stuck with her and that she held on to. This perspective shift reframed her thinking about why some students may have participated more, acting performatively to impress her, versus less, feeling traumatized by prior experiences. This gave Anne more awareness of how to create a space where certain students dominated. It also helped her think through how intentional community agreements and community building—alongside explicit facilitation strategies—could result in more equitable participation patterns.

For Brian, one of his biggest shifts in perspective was recognizing that there could be a strong disconnect between one's own perceptions, and the reality of what happened in the classroom. Brian recognized that it was easy to walk away from the classroom with a positive impression simply because one or two interactions were positive, even though other students were being marginalized. Similarly, other participants came to believe that having the real data was a huge part of promoting change because it allowed people to move past just having their own gut impressions.

For Gwen, her participation shifted how she was thinking about equity. Initially, she felt that equity meant providing support to each student, but if students wanted not to participate, then it was best to leave them alone. Over time she moved toward trying to provide *equal* participation for all students. Finally, she adopted a reparations viewpoint, recognizing that minoritized students might deserve *more* opportunities to participate to account for historical inequities and injustices. Even though she recognized that she hadn't fully embraced this perspective in her teaching moves, this was something she continued to work toward. Of all participants, Gwen was the one who adopted this new perspective on equity the most strongly.

For Kelly, a key insight was relinquishing control to her students. Kelly described a disconnect between what she knew were best practices in counseling and working with clients and the way that she interacted with her students. As she engaged with the equity analytics, she learned to give more control to her students, stepping back and giving them time and agency to engage in small groups rather than trying to control the process through whole-class discussions.

Elayne developed a variety of new insights and perspectives into her classroom. She was very explicit about how her thinking on participation and learning had shifted. She also became more aware of her own biases, how her biases may impact her practices, and the ways that her current teaching techniques centered *her*. Like Kelly, she learned to relinquish more control to her students. Elayne's perspective continued to shift even after her participation, as she created new activities and adopted a strengths-based approach to addressing health inequities in racially minoritized communities.

Sam's biggest takeaway was the power of data. The iterative and data-driven approach of equity analytics is consistent with an engineering mindset, so there was instant resonance. In addition to the equity metrics from the learning community, Sam began to collect various forms of data through polls, tracking attendance, and so forth. These formative assessment practices also shifted his instruction; for example, when he would create additional breakout rooms for students who needed extra support.

COACHING COHORTS

Three of the participants profiled in this book took on roles as coaches in an equity learning community. None of them had formally served as mentors for other instructors prior to this experience. Nonetheless, the participants drew upon a variety of their experiences to serve as coaches for their faculty peers. Of course, their prior experiences in equity learning communities provided them with practical knowledge of the program and helped promote buy-in from participants because the coaches could relate to their participants' experiences. In addition, the participants drew upon a variety of leadership roles that they had adopted in their communities.

For Brian and Kelly, although they were not educational researchers, they both had some familiarity with the field. Brian had been a mathematician for a long time and was involved in several mathematics-education efforts to improve his teaching, support equity, and understand theoretical foundations of learning. All this expertise was to his advantage, and both instructors in his community spoke openly about how knowledgeable they thought he was. For Kelly, she had knowledge of education, critical pedagogies, special education, and the K–12 schooling system, which were all to her advantage. She had a clear understanding of educational theories, even if she wasn't using them in her research. These skills set her up to be a very effective coach. Nonetheless, these background experiences are not prerequisite to success in coaching. Although his coaching was not profiled here, Sam had a variety of leadership experiences in engineering that he was able to leverage.

The coaches also received monetary support to do this work (described more in the next section). Another form of support that the faculty coaches had was the student coders. Although they were not profiled directly in this book, the student coders were *central* to the process. Both Marie and Jerome were responsible for suggesting some of the concrete strategies that were taken up by Anne and Gwen. In fact, although Brian was the figurehead of his group, most of the strategies taken up by his participants came from Marie. In Kelly's group, Jerome provided essential knowledge of mathematics to complement Kelly's counseling skills. In their debrief interviews, all the coaches acknowledged the strengths and incredible importance of the student coders. Working through different combinations of coaches and students is one way to support an effective process.

Finally, the coaching community itself provided guidance for each of the coaches. For example, Kelly appreciated the interdisciplinarity of the approach and felt that she learned a lot from her colleagues. In the coaching community space, each of the coaching teams was able to share their experiences and strategies and build community with other coaches. This in-it-togetherness was a key element of supporting the coaches persist while doing this difficult work. Moreover, in the coaching community space, I was able to share my expertise and concrete strategies with the coaching teams to support them in working more effectively with their faculty mentees.

INSTITUTIONALIZATION

The goal of bringing on prior participants as coaches was to decentralize control and work toward building a scalable model that can be used on any campus. What does all this mean for your campus? Here, I walk through a possible scenario for how your campus might adopt equity learning communities. Fortunately for you, these methods have been worked out, and this book, as well as my book on equitable teaching strategies, is a powerful resource that you can use to support rolling out this model.[1]

The first cohort of an equity learning community program is the most difficult one to start. If people in the local context are unfamiliar with the process, they may be less likely to sign up. Later, after there have been multiple cohorts, prior participants can help support recruiting future participants, and they also can act as spokespeople to provide a positive endorsement from their learning in the program. In my experiences, prior participants have played a strong role for recruiting others *and* generating interest and buy-in.

Another challenge for the initial cohort is developing the needed coaching skills. This isn't insurmountable but is a possible opportunity to work with an external consultant to learn the methods, at least the first time around. A good candidate for an initial facilitator would be somebody working in a Center for Teaching and Learning or Equity Advancement Office. After a few semesters of implementation, there will be a wealth of local expertise and knowledge to support future iterations.

In three of the cases above, faculty were recruited to serve as coaches following their participation in the program. Brian participated for one semester, Kelly for two semesters, and Sam for three semesters. The additional time that Kelly and Sam spent as participants is commensurate with their relatively junior status in the field. Although he only participated in an equity learning community for one semester, Brian had taught for over a decade and had a wealth of other experiences to draw from. It is highly recommended that coaches participate in the program themselves before coaching. In fact, even Niral and I, who developed this process, have made sure to spend time coding our own classroom practices and reflecting on equity metrics.

As each coach works with cohorts of new instructors, it provides opportunities to recruit new instructors to serve as future coaches. Scaling up the model in this way allows for sustained growth as new instructors do work, and it allows spreading across different disciplinary contexts.

As a campus, there are a variety of ways to support this growth. First, monetary incentives are one way to recognize that the institution values this work. In my work, instructors received $750 per semester, and coaches received $1,500. When one considers that instructors spent only five hours in meetings (distributed over the semester) and coaches spent nine hours in meetings (with additional coaching meetings between debriefs), the compensation of at least one hundred dollars per hour was reasonable. It is the ongoing data-driven support that makes the process so efficient. Of course, additional time and energy goes into thinking about the process, reflecting on instruction, and trying new practices, but there are no formal constraints on when faculty participants do that work, and they can incorporate it into their regular planning activities.

The final element is the student coding team. In my work, graduate students have played a valuable role in collecting data, coding, and providing feedback. An institution can certainly recruit students (undergraduate or graduate) to do this work. A benefit of this approach is that it provides professional learning for students, but a downside is that there is a constant rotation of students that need to be familiar with the coding methods. Another option is to use salaried staff members (e.g., in a Center for Teaching and Learning) to spend some of their time coding. This allows individuals to build expertise over time and continue to enhance their coding, feedback, and coaching skills. The coders should always participate in the coaching sessions because they are the ones who have the most intimate knowledge of what happened in the classroom of the participating faculty member.

CLOSING

Here we are, at the end of the cases. We've seen how six instructors positively transformed their perspectives and pedagogies and reduced gender and racial inequities of participation in their classrooms. Yet, equity learning communities are not panaceas, and just as the instructors made progress, there remains work to do. None of the instructors *eliminated* inequities through their work. Fortunately, even after their equity learning community disbands, participants often continue to transform their instruction to address the ongoing challenges of pervasive inequities in our education system.

These are just six of many instructors who have been a part of equity learning communities. In contrast to just "talking about equity," participants have done the hard work to really reflect on their teaching. As one participant who wasn't part of this book shared,

> Check your ego at the door. You're going to find some very interesting insights that may be difficult to swallow but are very productive. After going through this program, I've developed a lot of practices that I'm still using today.

Equity learning communities go beyond **equity talk** to address inequities on college campuses in a way that faculty can relate to and act upon.

Now, I invite you the reader to take up this work. I imagine that you picked up this book because you have the goal of teaching more equitably or supporting others to do so. Drawing on the key ideas in this book—the use of data, collaborative learning, and incremental change—you now have concrete strategies to enhance classroom equity. Transforming education to be more equitable is imperative, as we work to create a more just and democratic future for generations to come.

Acknowledgments

This book was only possible with the wisdom, experience, and support of dear colleagues, friends, and collaborators. I thank Molly Cerrone and the editorial team at Harvard Education Press for substantial feedback that has helped shape the work. I also thank all those who read and provided feedback on drafts of the book, including Niral Shah, Aileen Reid, Liza Bondurant, Sam Ridgway, and all the participants in this study who read their case studies. I thank Suparna Kure for her help creating the equity learning community flowchart diagram. While I was the principal investigator of the research in this book, the foundations of this work were built in collaboration with others. Here I acknowledge the foundational contributions of others to this work.

To Niral Shah, this work is fundamentally *our* work. Together, we built EQUIP and learned how to help instructors use data as the basis for change. I still remember talking about our shared vision over a decade ago, to focus our careers on work with a concrete impact on students in schools. I couldn't ask for a better collaborator and friend. I hope that our work together continues for years to come.

To Robin Wilson, you made me believe in EQUIP, and you made me believe in myself. You've always been a role model for the type of mathematician and educator that I want to be. To Cathery Yeh, our friendship and collaborations have brought hope, life, and energy to the work for many years now. I'm so grateful for how you keep pushing me in my thinking.

To Vicki Hand, who was one of the very first people to directly support this work and believe in its promise. To Rachel Lotan, for her tireless championship of equitable classrooms, and for all her support of my work.

To the countless others who have contributed to EQUIP—by using the tool, citing the work, encouraging me to keep going—I am deeply moved by you. To the participants in this book—you know who you are, but I can't name you here—you've given us all a gift by being vulnerable in opening your classrooms and sharing your learning with the world. I dedicate this work to you.

Appendix A: Methods

This chapter focuses on the methods underlying this study. I provide as much detail as needed to help a reader understand the selection of participants, data collection, coding of observations, and provision of data to instructors.

PARTICIPANTS

This project was funded primarily by a National Science Foundation CAREER grant, which focused on improving equitable teaching in postsecondary STEM contexts. Given that I was working at San Diego State University at the time of writing this book, I was primarily connected into educator networks in California. For example, I had opportunities to work with faculty in the California State University system, as well as with regional networks in Southern California. I used both as avenues for recruitment. As a result, the six focal instructors were all located in California. The instructors spanned a total of four institutions. Elayne, Kelly, and Sam were all at the same institution. It was a PhD-granting institution that was research intensive but also teaching focused. Anne was at an elite liberal arts college. Brian was at a master's-granting institution. Gwen was at a private PhD-granting university. In other studies, I have worked across the US at a variety of different locations.

Brian initially participated in fall 2018 as a part of pilot work that preceded the CAREER grant. He was later recruited to serve as a coach for the CAREER project. The rest of the participants were all recruited through open calls. Sam began in spring 2020 and continued through the next academic year (fall 2020 to spring 2021) as a participant. Both Kelly and Elayne received one-on-one coaching during the same year (fall 2020 to spring 2021). Sam, Brian, and Kelly all served as coaches during the next year (Fall 2021 to spring 2022), and this was the same year that both Anne and Gwen were recruited. Anne worked with Brian as a coach, and Gwen worked with Kelly as a coach. In table A.1, I provide an overview of the courses that each instructor taught during each semester.

TABLE A.1 Courses taught by each of the focal instructors

Instructor	*Course Name*	*Description*	*Date*	*Num. Obs.*	*Excluded*
Anne	Linear Algebra	Matrices, vector spaces, and associated operations.	Fall 2021	4	
Anne	Mathematical Modeling	A lab course with interactive programming and troubleshooting.	Spring 2022	3	Nontraditional course. Observations all within a 2-week period; no revision.
Brian	Calculus	Introductory calculus for math- and STEM-intensive majors.	Fall 2018	5	
Elayne*	Public Health and Behavioral Science	Health behaviors, needs assessment, program design.	Fall 2020	3	
Elayne*	Public Health and Behavioral Science	Health behaviors, needs assessment, program design.	Spring 2021	5	
Gwen	Math for Social Justice		Fall 2021	4	
Gwen	Upper-Division Math Seminar		Spring 2022	3	Only 5 students. Discussions focused on supporting a single disabled student.
Kelly*	School Counseling Program Development	ASCA framework to build a school counseling program.	Fall 2020	7	
Kelly*	Learning, Achievement, and Instruction	Design, instruction, and assessment for school counseling curriculum.	Spring 2021	2	
Sam*	Civil Engineering Design	Water systems and other civil engineering topics.	Spring 2020	5	
Sam*	Civil Engineering Design	Water systems and other civil engineering topics.	Fall 2020	5	
Sam*	Civil Engineering Design	Water systems and other civil engineering topics.	Spring 2021	3	

*Instructors with an asterisk taught in a virtual, synchronous setting. Other instructors were in face-to-face classrooms.

DATA SOURCES

The data for this book came from a variety of sources. Below, I outline each of the main data sources: (1) classroom observations, (2) interviews, (3) debrief sessions, and (4) coaching meetings.

Classroom observations

Three of the instructors in the study (Anne, Gwen, and Brian) all taught in face-to-face classrooms. Because these instructors were working remotely from us, in each case, they set up a single stationary camera in the front of the room while they were teaching. This camera was aimed at the students rather than the instructor so that we could capture student participation. The camera did a good job of capturing the whole class, allowing us to code over 95 percent of student contributions. Students who opted out of the study sat in a place that was not captured by the camera. Notably, fewer than two students opted out in any given classroom.

After recording the classroom video, the instructors uploaded it using cloud-based services (like Google Drive) so that our team could code the data. Ideally, the instructors would upload the video two weeks before the next debrief meeting, to allow for our team to code the video, generate feedback, send the feedback, and have time for the instructors to process the feedback. This ideal wasn't always met in practice. In particular, instructors were more likely to fall off the recording schedule as more semesters went by, which is one reason that we did not include data for the second semester from many instructors.

Alongside the video recordings, instructors shared a photo roster of their classes with us to facilitate identifying students in the videos. In some cases, instructors could generate this directly from their institution, or they did it as a part of their own pedagogical practices. In other cases, our coding team took screenshots of the classroom videos and had the instructor identify any students who participated that we could not identify.

For the instructors who taught in synchronous virtual environments (all of them used Zoom), we used the cloud-recording functionality of Zoom. This allowed for an instructor to easily send their videos directly to us, and an added benefit was that Zoom automatically identified which participant was speaking at any time, which facilitated EQUIP coding. One instructor, Sam, also recorded some of his breakout sessions using the local-recording function. We only debriefed one of these recordings, during the spring 2020 semester. Given that

Sam infrequently recorded the breakouts, and they were not a major focus of the professional development, they are removed from the larger sample to allow for easier comparability across instructors.

Interviews

With each participating instructor, we conducted intake and exit interviews. As described previously, the intake interviews served a variety of purposes from building rapport to getting to know the instructor and, finally, for customizing data analytics. In addition, we conducted exit interviews with each instructor. These interviews took place the semester following the last semester that the instructor was involved in the program. This allowed us to ask questions about how instructors continued to use teaching practices even after their formal participation was completed.

Debrief sessions

To understand participants' learning processes and the coaching process, we recorded all debrief meetings between participants and their coaches. These debrief meetings all took place over Zoom, and we used the cloud-recording functionality.[1] With Brian, Kelly, Elayne, and Sam, I personally served as the coach. Later, Brian was a coach for Anne, and Kelly was a coach for Gwen. These data showing how former participants were able to take up the coaching role helped us understand the scalability of our approach.

Coaching meetings

During Fall 2021 to spring 2022, Brian, Kelly, and Sam all served as coaches. To support them in doing this work, I organized monthly coaching meetings between the coaching team and the coding team. The purpose of these meetings was to provide support and surface any issues that the coaches were encountering. It also allowed the coaches to provide peer support to one another as they learned to take on this new role. Again, these were virtual meetings, and they were all recorded for future analysis. To be clear, other than in the intake interviews, I personally had no direct contact with participants during the fall 2021 to spring 2022 academic year. The coaches and their student assistants were responsible for all direct support.

Other data sources

Finally, we collected a variety of other data sources for each instructor. We collected and archived feedback forms, EQUIP data, and any relevant classroom artifacts from each of the instructors. When used in conjunction with a variety of recordings, all these data allowed us to construct a holistic picture of their practice and learning processes.

SETTING UP EQUIP

To instantiate the equity-analytics approach, we used the EQUIP observation tool, and particularly the EQUIP web app (www.equip.ninja). The web app was a convenient tool for setting up classrooms for each of the participating instructors, and the app also automatically generated the data analytics that were used in this study. Setting up the classrooms for each instructor involved gathering information about social-marker dimensions, creating a classroom roster, and choosing discourse dimensions. Each process is outlined in turn.

In the present study, the primary method for gathering student social-marker data was through electronic surveys. Our surveys typically included a mix of multiple-choice or free-response questions, depending on instructor preference.

In this study, we aimed to have three-to-five discourse dimensions for professional development. I focused almost exclusively on whole-group interactions (except for Ramesh who focused only on small groups for a whole semester). Nonetheless, for some of the virtual classrooms we did code breakouts, and for one of the instructors (not profiled here) the entire study focused on small-group interactions. Overall, in our research and professional-development work we can focus on the modality that the instructor desires, but it happens in this case we focused mostly on whole-class interactions. Here, I provide detail about some of the most important EQUIP dimensions used in the study (see table A.2).

Student talk length

The *student talk length* dimension focuses on the length of any given student contribution. Typically, this is coded with levels of *1–4 words*, *5–20 words,* and *21+ words*. The category *1–4 words* is typical of IRE sequences, in which students provide only short answers and rarely get to explain their thinking.[2] In contrast, longer contributions are indicative of deeper opportunities to

TABLE A.2 Dimensions of EQUIP

Dimension	*Levels*
Student talk length	21 or more words
	5–20 words
	1–4 words
Student talk type	Why
	How
	What
	Other
Teacher solicitation method	Called on
	Not called on
Teacher solicitation type	Why
	How
	What
	Other
	N/A
Teacher explicit evaluation	Yes
	No

participate. The categories of 5–20 words and 21+ words roughly correspond to a single sentence and multiple sentences. In studies where EQUIP is used in real-time (or without video or a transcript), it can be more productive to use categories such as *a few words, one sentence,* and *multiple sentences.*

The length of talk is consequential for at least two reasons. First, when students can discuss their thinking at length, it provides them with meaningful opportunities to learn. These are of different quality from only uttering a few words at a time. In addition, *length of talk* can provide insight into which individual students and groups of students are taking up more space in classroom discussion. This is consequential for both identity development through participation and how other students in the class will perceive one another. Research suggests that high-level participation is important for all students, and further, opportunities to talk at length are particularly important for supporting the language development of emergent multilingual students.[3]

Student talk type

In addition to the length of talk, the *student talk type* is of consequence for understanding the quality of participation. In general, when students explain their thinking, it is viewed as a higher form of cognition that is more valuable for learning than simply providing an answer.[4] Our work has utilized a hierarchy of *Why, How, What,* and *Other,* which corresponds to research in both science education and math education.[5] Tracking the types of participation from different students can provide valuable insights into teacher biases; for instance, when they highlight how some students may be perceived as capable of participating only at lower levels. In our prior work, we have seen that low-level questions can even be used as a disciplinary tactic to keep students "engaged," but they do not really allow them to meaningfully participate.

Teacher solicitation method

Teacher solicitation method focuses on how students are brought into the conversation to participate. In general, we contrast between instances when students are explicitly *called on* with when they are *not called on* and participate spontaneously. In our research, we find that students who are historically advantaged in a discipline are most likely to respond when *not called on*, as they feel a sense of agency and entitlement. Thus, an instructor needs to be intentional about how they bring students into the conversation to promote equity. There is always a tension between instructor-moderated discourse (with more *called-on* talk), and more free-flowing discourse (with more *not-called-on talk*), as the latter is susceptible to inequity but also signifies greater student agency. It is upon the instructor to create a strong classroom community and communication agreements that can promote equitable *not-called-on* talk.

Teacher solicitation type

Corresponding to the different student talk types, a teacher might ask different types of questions that are looking for different types of talk. Lower-level *What* questions typically focus on getting to the answer but may remove the challenge of deeper thinking. In contrast, higher-level *Why* questions can press students to explain their thinking. In this way, the overall quality of questions is a matter of equity. In a classroom that only focuses on getting answers, most students are prevented from deeper thinking. But even when there are high-level questions, they need to be distributed in an equitable way.

Teacher explicit evaluation

Teacher explicit evaluation focuses on what a teacher does with student ideas when they come out into the public space. Are they evaluated or simply left open for other students to respond to? In general, it is seen as valuable when teachers use moves such as revoicing to allow other students to engage with one another, rather than acting as a central authority.[6] When students can act as authorities, it helps them develop productively as learners.[7]

Coding with EQUIP

The process of coding is best illustrated by working through some quick examples. Here, I sample some actual transcripts (deidentified) from algebra classrooms in one of our studies. Neither the details nor the mathematics nor the specific lessons are important for understanding these short coding examples. Our goal here is to look at the types of talk from the teacher and students and how we would code it using EQUIP.

The first example comes from a classroom that was discussing the volume of various solids. Here we provide a segment of the transcript.

TEACHER: The volume of a rectangular prism was one of the first formulas that was talked about in the book. Can someone tell me what the answer was for number three?

JOSEF: 120

TEACHER: How did you find 120?

JOSEF: I did five times six times four.

TEACHER: Correct. It was length times width times height in no particular order.

TEACHER: Next, what was the estimate for the volume of a pyramid? Alex?

ALEX: Um, I think it is the same as a cone, because the relationship between a rectangular cylinder and a cone seems like it would be the same for a prism and a pyramid. So it's forty.

TEACHER: Who agrees with Alex? Okay, Edgar, what did you say?

EDGAR: Oh, wait, sorry. I don't know the answer.

TEACHER: Oh, okay. How about Alexander?

ALEXANDER: Yeah, I got a different answer because I thought the pyramid was just one-half of the rectangular prism.

CHARLIE: I got sixty.

TEACHER: Charlie, why did you think that?

CHARLIE: It's kinda like a rectangle, and a triangle, so you divide it by two to get the area of the other one.

TEACHER: Did anyone else get a different answer?

EDGAR: I got eighty because I tried like the relationship between a sphere and a cylinder.

TEACHER: Oh, so you thought it was like two-thirds.

EDGAR: Yeah.

TEACHER: So it turns out that Alex was correct, thinking about one-third. [. . .]

The first step to coding this segment is to break it up into separate contributions. The key thing to remember is that each time a new student talked it was considered a new contribution. This means that the above discussion has a total of six contributions. We next break down the contributions and how they were coded, one by one.

Contribution one

Transcript	*Coding*
Teacher: The volume of a rectangular prism was one of the first formulas that was talked about in the book. Can someone tell me what the answer was for number three? Josef: 120 Teacher: How did you find 120? Josef: I did five times six times four. Teacher: Correct. It was length times width times height in no particular order.	Talk length: *5–20 words* Talk type: *How* Solicitation method: *Not called on* Solicitation type: *How* Explicit evaluation: *Yes*

The first contribution consisted of back-and-forth between the instructor and Josef. The longest segment of talk from Josef was seven words, fitting in the *5–20 words* category. Josef initially provides an answer (*What* talk), but later he describes his process for finding the answer, which is considered a *How* statement. Josef initially volunteers the answer without explicitly being called on, so it is *not called on*. Like Josef, the teacher initially asks *what* the answer is, but later follows up asking *how* to get to the answer, so it is *How* for the solicitation type. Finally, the teacher says, "Correct," which is an explicit evaluation of Josef's answer.

Contribution two

Transcript	*Coding*
Teacher: Next, what was the estimate for the volume of a pyramid? Alex? Alex: Um, I think it is the same as a cone, because the relationship between a rectangular cylinder and a cone seems like it would be the same for a prism and a pyramid. So it's forty.	Talk length: *21+ words* Talk type: *Why* Solicitation method: *Called on* Solicitation type: *What* Explicit evaluation: *Yes*

The second contribution is between the teacher and Alex. In this case, Alex has well over *21+ words*. Here the teachers asks *what* the estimate is, but Alex goes deeper to explain *why* he had a particular answer. Alex is directly *called on* by the teacher. Although it doesn't happen yet, at the very end of the episode (after more students contribute), the teacher explicitly evaluates Alex's answer as being correct when she says, "So it turns out that Alex was correct, thinking about one-third."

Contribution three

Transcript	*Coding*
Teacher: Who agrees with Alex? Okay, Edgar, what did you say? Edgar: Oh, wait, sorry. I don't know the answer.	Talk length: *5–20 words* Talk type: *Other* Solicitation method: *Called on* Solicitation type: *Other* Explicit evaluation: *No*

In this next episode, the teacher *calls on* Edgar, asking a nonmathematical question that is coded as *Other*. Edgar responds with *5–20 words*, stating that he doesn't know the answer, which is an *Other* type of statement. There is *no* evaluation.

Contribution four

Transcript	*Coding*
Teacher: Oh, okay. How about Alexander? Alexander: Yeah, I got a different answer because I thought the pyramid was just one-half of the rectangular prism.	Talk length: *5–20 words* Talk type: *Why* Solicitation method: *Called on* Solicitation type: *Other* Explicit evaluation: *No*

Here, the teacher *calls on* Alexander, with an *Other* type of question, because it is just a general solicitation. Alexander responds with *5–20 words*, explaining in-depth *why* he got a different answer. Again, there is *no* teacher evaluation.

Contribution five

Transcript	*Coding*
Charlie: I got sixty. Teacher: Charlie, why did you think that? Charlie: It's kinda like a rectangle, and a triangle, so you divide it by two to get the area of the other one.	Talk length: *21+ words* Talk type: *Why* Solicitation method: *Not called on* Solicitation type: *Why* Explicit evaluation: *No*

Here, Charlie offers the answer, sixty, while *not called on*. Although there was initially no teacher question, the follow-up question asked Charlie to explain *why*, and Charlie responds with a *Why* explanation of *21+ words*. There is *no* teacher evaluation.

Contribution six

Transcript	*Coding*
Teacher: Did anyone else get a different answer? Edgar: I got eighty because I tried like the relationship between a sphere and a cylinder. Teacher: Oh, so you thought it was like two-thirds. Edgar: Yeah. Teacher: So it turns out that Alex was correct, thinking about one-third.	Talk length: *5–20 words* Talk type: *Why* Solicitation method: *Not called on* Solicitation type: *Other* Explicit evaluation: *Yes*

The last contribution returns to Edgar. Here, Edgar responds to the teacher's repeated solicitations to bring in more students (of type *Other)*, but he is *not called on* because the teacher doesn't directly choose him to share. Edgar describes *why* he got a different answer, in *5–20 words*. The teacher does evaluate the response, by revealing it is not two-thirds but Alex's response of one-third that was correct. Here the evaluation was coded *Yes* (and not above in contribution five), because it comes immediately after Edgar's contribution.

These short examples of coding are not intended to replace the multiple days of coding practice we use to train researchers or coaches. Rather, they are provided as examples to show the reader what EQUIP coding looks like in general. In any given context, the users will want to start with the general EQUIP codes and approach and build a consensus understanding on their own data, which could look very different. When multiple people are providing coaching or doing coding, it is best for them to code some of the same segments of classroom practice so that they can all gain a common understanding and even collect examples of what defines each code in their context.

The short examples also highlight the types of data EQUIP can provide. For instance, we note that all six contributions above were by boys in the class. One would have to code more to make any strong claims, but here we see the possible start of a pattern of gender marginalization for girls in the class. We see that there are a variety of different types of contributions, but most of them are only at the *5–20 words* level. This indicates that students are giving relatively short responses, but at least they are explaining their thinking in full sentences. After coding the lesson in its entirety, it would be possible to generate deeper data analytics to provide the teacher with data for reflection.

Appendix B: Sample Protocols and Materials

SAMPLE SCHEDULE

To create an effective learning environment for mentees, the goal is to have three to four debrief sessions. In between these debriefs, it is important for the coaching team to meet. This could result in the following sample schedule:

- Week 1: August 23 (First week of classes—No meeting)
- Meeting 1 (Week 3): September 7 (Onboarding coaches)
- Meeting 2 (Week 6): September 28 (Discuss debrief 1)
- Meeting 3 (Week 9): October 19 (Discuss debrief 2)
- Meeting 4 (Week 12): November 9 (Discuss debrief 3)
- Meeting 5 (Week 15): December 7 (Discuss debrief 4)

It is ideal if the coaching team can hold an hour-long time slot open in their calendars so that these meetings can be shifted as needed. In practice things don't always line up with the ideal. For example, if one of the observations happens late or something else comes up, the team might want to shift one of our meetings by a week (earlier or later).

Assuming that we do have those five meeting times, the goal would be to perform an observation/debrief in between our sessions. Thus, the observation/debrief windows with participants would be as follows:

- Debrief 1: September 7–September 28
- Debrief 2: September 28–October 19
- Debrief 3: October 19–November 9
- Debrief 4: November 9–December 7

In some cases, only three debrief meetings will happen. If only one or two debriefs were to happen, it would be a threat to the validity and efficacy of this program in supporting mentees to teach equitably.

CLASS INTRODUCTION SCRIPT

Hi, everyone! I wanted to let you know that this semester I am participating in a project to help me improve my teaching. The overall goal of the project is to better understand how to promote equitable teaching in STEM classrooms and to ensure that all students have meaningful opportunities to learn. I am part of a cohort with other instructors across the country who are all working together to improve our education system.

As a part of the project, I will be recording my teaching several times throughout the year. These recordings will only be shared with the research team who will then generate analytics to help me better understand what is happening in the classroom and adjust my teaching accordingly. None of your identifying information will be shared, and the videos will only be used by the research team to promote better teaching. The project is governed by an Institutional Review Board and code of ethics to ensure that everyone is protected.

Of course, it is completely optional for you to participate in the study. To participate, you don't have to do anything special; you just show up and engage in class as you normally would. If you are uncomfortable with the video camera or don't want to be recorded, you can fill out the opt-out form, and we will respect your privacy when the video camera is on by seating you in a different place in the room. Whether or not you participate will have no impact on your grade whatsoever. Of course, we do appreciate your allowing us to include you in the study, because ultimately this is what helps us (and others) get better at teaching.

I will also hand out a short demographic survey that will provide us information for the study. I would appreciate it if you could fill this out, but again, your participation is totally optional and does not affect your grade.

INTAKE INTERVIEW (PARTICIPANTS)

Instructor background

1. Briefly, can you tell me about your discipline and the work that you do?
2. How long have you been teaching? How long at this institution?
3. Describe a typical day in your classroom.
    a. How would your students describe your style as a teacher?
    b. What things are you really good at as a teacher? What things are you still working on?

On equity (in general)

1. What does *equity* mean to you?
2. How do you think about equity in terms of your teaching?
   a. What kinds of things do you do to foster equity in your classroom?
   b. Does this show up in your curriculum or assessment practices?
3. Have you seen inequities come up in your classroom in the past?
   a. How did you respond?
4. What are your equity goals for this semester?
   a. How does this relate to other things you're doing as a teacher?

On gender equity

1. What is your gender identity? Can you think of a time in your personal or professional life where your gender identity was salient to you?
2. How do you think gender affects students in your discipline?
3. Are there gender stereotypes in your discipline?
   a. Why do you think these stereotypes exist?
4. Can you think of a time when something related to gender came up in your class?
   a. In general, how do you think about gender in your teaching? (This could be your gender or your students' genders.)
   b. Do you have particular teaching strategies to promote gender equity or concerns that you watch out for?
5. Has the way you think about gender changed over time?

On racial equity

1. What is your racial/ethnic identity? Can you think of a time in your personal or professional life where your racial/ethnic identity was salient to you?
2. How do you think race affects students in your discipline?
3. Are there racial stereotypes in your discipline?
   a. Why do you think these stereotypes exist?
4. Can you think of a time when something related to race came up in your class?
   a. In general, how do you think about race in your teaching? (This could be your race or your students' races.)

   b. Do you have particular teaching strategies to promote racial equity or concerns that you watch out for?
5. Has the way you think about race changed over time?

Closing

1. Is there anything in particular we should pay attention to in your classroom this semester? (Standard EQUIP dimensions will look for teacher questions, student talk type, and student talk length. Standard demographics are race and gender.)
2. What else should I know that I haven't asked?

INTAKE INTERVIEW (COACHES)

1. Why are you interested in this program? What do you hope to gain from it?
2. What are your prior experiences with coaching/mentoring?
   a. As a coach/mentor?
   b. As a mentee?
3. What do you think is the role of a coach/mentor?
   a. What do you think is the role of a mentee?
4. What was one of your best experiences either as a mentor or a mentee? How has that influenced your beliefs/approach toward mentorship?
5. What is your approach to coaching/mentorship?
   a. What are your goals for your mentees?
6. What would you consider to be success with the people you are coaching?
7. What types of support would you like to help you be a successful coach?
8. Do you have any preferences for creating a productive, accessible workflow together?
9. What else should we know?

DEBRIEF PROTOCOL

Framing: The goal with debrief meetings is to provide participants with an opportunity to reflect on inequities in their classrooms. In general, it is easier for people to reflect on gender inequities, while racial inequities are harder to confront. As a facilitator, we want to run the meeting in a way that avoids blaming or defensiveness. We want to avoid using any judgmental language like *bad*, *prob-*

lematic, *failing*, and so forth. Rather, we can notice patterns that are a work in progress and that can still be changed with effort.

Thus, we need to create an open, trusting environment that allows for vulnerability. It is important that we reassure mentees that these are hard issues that *everyone* is working on (even us), and seeing a pattern of inequity doesn't say something bad about us as people. It just means we have more work to do to confront systems of oppression in society. This is hard work, and we don't usually get to see what happens in our classroom, which is why we are doing this whole thing together as a team.

When reflecting on data, it is best to first let the mentee make any observations about what they notice and continue from there. Our goal is to build on what the mentee is doing and what they can improve rather than imposing our ideas on them. But we still have some role in nudging folks to notice patterns they wouldn't otherwise.

In general, people are less attuned to social-marker inequities in the beginning and are ready to explain them away in terms of individual characteristics. It's also easier for people to see individual students as dominant or not participating rather than seeing groups of students based on racialized, gendered, or otherwise identity-related phenomena. We want to move people in this direction, but we also need to build sufficient trust that we can provide this information without it becoming a confrontation.

Initial questions

1. How are things going in your classroom? Anything notable that you want to share?
   a. What's going well? What could be better?
2. What have you been working on over the past few weeks (in terms of strategies and equity)? Can we talk about how that is going?
3. Okay, let's focus on the data; What patterns did you notice?
4. Do you notice anything overall, big picture?

Probing phase

After asking some initial questions, if a participant is not seeing the inequities in the data, this is the place to start gently nudging by making them aware of some patterns you noticed. This can be done by initially asking somewhat leading questions and then adding in your own observations. Here are some sample questions:

1. Let's look at gender patterns. Do you notice anything?
   a. Follow up—I noticed . . .
2. Let's look at racialized patterns. Do you notice anything?
   a. Follow up—I noticed . . .
3. Let's look at patterns in social marker X. Do you notice anything?
   a. Follow up—I noticed . . .
4. Let's look at individual student patterns. Do you notice anything?
   a. Follow up—I noticed . . .

Action plans

After spending time looking at patterns of inequity, the goal is to focus on possible teaching strategies the instructor can use to adjust the patterns to be more equitable next time. In general, it is recommended that an instructor focuses on one (or at most two) different types of inequities they want to shift. And the instructor should practice just one change to their practice between cycles (or possibly two changes if the changes to teaching are incredibly minor).

Here are some of the types of changes that instructors might make:

1. If an instructor uses primarily *What* type questions, they can focus on adding in more *Why* questions. While this is good pedagogical practice in general, it is unlikely to shift patterns of inequitable participation.
2. The instructor can explicitly get students to raise their hands and have "five hands up" before calling on someone. This is one of the most important changes for instructors who have no deliberate way to solicit participation. If students simply shout out answers, they will always have inequitable patterns.
3. Using a turn-and-talk or think-pair-share to create partner talk, listening to students during the partner-work time, and then intentionally selecting specific minoritized students to share their ideas in the whole-class discussion.
4. Deeper strategies like the five practices or assigning competence can work even further to improve equitable teaching.[1]

It's important that before the end of the meeting, the mentee picks a particular pattern they want to shift and a particular strategy they are going to use to try to shift it. This provides accountability, something that you can check in on during the next meeting as they talk about what they are working on.

DEMOGRAPHIC QUESTIONNAIRE (FOR STUDENTS)

Thank you for your participation in our study. Ultimately, the purpose of this study is to provide feedback to your teacher so that they can enhance your learning experience and ensure that all learners are having a meaningful opportunity to engage. By filling out information on this form, you will be helping your instructor create a more positive learning environment. No identifying information will be shared outside of the research team, who is bound by a code of ethics and an Institutional Review Board.

1. What is your name?
2. What is your instructor's name?
3. What is your gender identity?
4. What is your racial/ethnic identity?
5. Are there any other important things about your identity you would like to share?

THE EQUIP CODEBOOK

In this last section of the book, I provide a codebook for a set of the standard EQUIP dimensions. We recognize that users may always choose their own dimensions because EQUIP is fully customizable, but this gives a starting point that users may wish to build from.

Identifying new contributions

The basic unit of analysis in EQUIP is called a *contribution*. A contribution consists of any string of utterances from a single student. As soon as a new student contributes, it forms a new participation sequence. If a single student speaks back and forth with the teacher but no other students participate, then this whole interaction is counted as a part of the same contribution.

There are several reasons that the unit of analysis is defined in this way. First, because EQUIP generates disaggregated analytics, it means that any coding that happens must be able to be tied to a specific student. With student talk, it is clear that it belongs to that particular student. As far as teacher actions are concerned, they must be attributed to a particular student that they are interacting with so that they can be coded. Thus, coding is segmented in a way so that all segmenting takes place with respect to students, constituting new contributions, and then coding is tied to that particular contribution. This allows the coded events to be disaggregated and aggregated in a number of different ways.

Second, we allow for multiple back-and-forth turns between a teacher and a single student because this reflects our understanding of the discussion moves that teachers use in real classrooms. Very often, teachers may start with a simple question, like asking for an answer, and then follow up by asking a student to explain their process and, finally, justify why the answer is correct. Our goal is to capture this whole interaction as a single contribution and to code a high level of teacher questioning and student response. Otherwise, if we were to code all the smaller, intermediate questions in the middle, we might instead paint a picture of a teacher's teaching that didn't fully capture the richness of the discourse moves. Ultimately this was a design decision in the development of EQUIP. As a result, classrooms in which students have a large number of discussions back and forth with each other will have relatively more contributions coded than classrooms in which discourse is more teacher-centric.

Third, we segment new contributions when a new student is involved because it gives us a concrete, relatively unambiguous way to mark new contributions. Still, we recognize, for instance, that if a single student were dominating a classroom discussion, they might contribute a few ideas that would all be considered part of the same interaction. For this reason, we suggest that users choose a certain amount of time (e.g., one or two minutes) as a cutoff between contributions. Following this logic, if a teacher interacted with a student named Dan, then lectured for one minute, and then interacted with Dan again, this would be counted as two contributions, both for the student Dan. The appropriate interval of time would depend on the circumstances and the particular goals of a project.

EQUIP coding relies upon identifying a student who participates, so if a participant can't be identified, no contribution is coded. Suppose again that a student Dan is in a conversation back and forth with the teacher. If an unnamed or unidentifiable student speaks and then Dan continues to speak afterward, it would all be counted as one sequence because the unnamed student is ignored. Similarly, choral responses are ignored because there is no particular student who is making the contribution.

When coding videos, we also recognize that side talk between students might be captured. Suppose a video camera is sitting in the back of a classroom. This may capture talk at a nearby table. However, for the purposes of coding whole-class discussion, we would ignore this side talk because it is not public. If a team has different goals, such as coding a small group, then such talk may be included. Similarly, if a teacher has a side conversation with just one student, we would not capture that because it is not public. Or, if two students talk to one another during a think-pair-share or turn-and-talk move, it wouldn't be coded, as it's not public. In general, when coding a whole-class discussion, we are looking for participation that is visible to most of the class because if participation is not seen by other students, it will not contribute to positioning students in the public space.

When coding, it is important to identify each student with a unique name. Typically, we would recommend using only first names or just student initials, to protect the privacy of the students involved. However, if multiple students have the same name, then appropriate pseudonyms or last names must be included.

Last, we recognize that some coding situations do not focus on whole-class discussions but could capture small groups, side talk, and so on. In such cases, the rules above about public participation would not apply. In general, small-group coding will result in far more contributions than a whole-class discussion because of the density of talk. Also, if the majority of interactions involve students without a teacher, in such situations it may be easiest to not use any teacher-focused dimensions.

Solicitation method

Summary description: *Solicitation method* refers to the action corresponding to the initiation of a new contribution. The primary distinction we are interested in is whether a student is responsible for beginning the interaction or whether the teacher begins the interaction.

Dimension levels

1. *Called on*—A teacher calls on a specific student or asks for a student to share their ideas.
2. *Not called on*—A student just starts talking without the teacher telling them to.

Explanation and examples. The purpose of the solicitation method is to understand under what circumstances the teacher is bringing particular groups of students into the conversation and under what circumstances particular students are just talking of their own volition. By looking at *not-called-on* talk, a teacher can gain insight into the general atmosphere of their classroom and which students feel most comfortable. Without explicit equity work, this will generally follow stereotypes within a discipline. By looking at *called-on* talk, a teacher can see how their implicit biases might play out; for instance, as they call on certain groups of students more than others.

Called on. This dimension is coded as *called on* if a teacher is in any way responsible for picking the student who talks. This could happen when a teacher calls on a student by name; says something like "Yes," "All right," or "Go ahead" to a student who has their hand up; or points, nods, or otherwise gestures in a way that provides the conversational floor to any particular student.

Not called on. This dimension is coded as *not called on* if a student makes a spontaneous comment or just starts talking on their own. The key idea is that the student initiates the contribution. Often, this could be in response to a teacher question. For instance, if the teacher asks, "What is the answer to this problem?" and a student shouts out the answer without being specifically asked to speak, it would be coded as *not called on*. In other cases, a student may just shout out a comment even without a teacher asking a question. This would be coded as *not called on* as well.

Example one: Calling on groups. If a teacher calls on a group to share—for example, by asking "Can someone in group one explain their thinking?"—we could code it as either *called on* or *not called on* according to what happens. If a particular student in that group then raises their hand after being prompted, we would code it as *called on*. However, if one student just shouts out, it would be coded as *not called on*. In this case, the teacher does some prompting to pick a particular group, but it is what happens next that depends on how it is coded. It would be possible for a user to develop a third-level *group* for the solicitation method code, but in our experience, this situation is not that common, so we typically favor having fewer codes overall.

Teacher solicitation type

Summary description: *Teacher solicitation type* refers to the type of question or task that a student is asked to engage with. The levels of this code are roughly aligned with different types of student talk or different levels of cognitive demand. When a student has multiple utterances within a single contribution, this dimension is coded for the *highest* level of student contribution, to account for the teacher pressing students to provide reasoning.

Dimension levels

1. Why—Teacher asks student to explain or justify their reasoning.
2. How—Teacher asks for a student's solution method.
3. What—Teacher asks a student to read part of a problem, recall a fact, or give a numerical or verbal answer.
4. Other—Teacher asks a general question (e.g., "What did you think?").
5. N/A—Teacher does not ask the student a question.

Explanation and examples. The purpose of the teacher solicitation dimension is to understand what question or task a student is responding to during a given contribution. Because there may be multiple questions asked in a single contribution, there are two guidelines used to determine how to code the dimension. First, when a teacher asks multiple questions in sequence, it is important to consider which question the teacher ultimately wants students to answer. Imagine a teacher is asking for the solution to a problem and says the following:

> This was a difficult problem. I would like for all of you to think about why the Pythagorean theorem works that way. Why do you think it works in this case? Let's look at the hypotenuse in this example. If the legs are of length three and four, what is the length of the hypotenuse?

In this segment, we see a teacher setting up a more general discussion about thinking about why the Pythagorean theorem works. However, the teacher quickly moves from this broader framing to ask a specific question about the length of the hypotenuse. This is a *What*-level question, and we would infer that ultimately this is the question the teacher is trying to get the students to respond to. In cases where it is slightly ambiguous which is the driving question from the teacher, it can be helpful to look at which question is ultimately taken up by the students.

Second, if there are multiple teacher solicitations during a single contribution, this dimension is coded to the highest level of solicitation, according to the following hierarchy: *Why* > *How* > *What* > *Other* > *N/A*. This hierarchy is in place to account for when a teacher uses multiple questions with a single student to help elicit their reasoning in more depth. Consider an exchange such as the following:

TEACHER: If the legs are of length 3 and 4, what is the length of the hypotenuse?
STUDENT: I got 5.
TEACHER: All right. How did you get that answer?
STUDENT: First, I took 3 and squared it, then I took 4 and squared it. So, I got 9 and 16. I added them together to get 25 and took the square root and got 5.

In this case, the teacher first asks the student what the answer was, but really this was just used as an entry point into asking the student how they got to the response. Thus, according to the hierarchy of *How* > *What*, the whole contribution would be coded as *How*.

Why. A *Why* solicitation aims to get a student to explain or justify their thinking about a particular answer, procedure, or concept. Within a teacher solicitation, key words to look out for include *explain*, *justify*, *prove*, *show why*, *give reasons for*, *how do you know*, or *why do you think*. While the presence of any of these words does not guarantee that there is a *Why* solicitation, they strongly suggest it. We see how these words play out in the following examples:

- "Explain what you figured out."
- "What do you need a three for?"
- "Who else heard what Lakeya said and can explain her strategy?"
- "How do you know that seven is the correct answer?"

Consider the phrase *How do you know*. Even though the word *how* is in the phrasing—because the question is about getting student reasoning out, not following a procedure—it is coded as a *Why* type of contribution.

How. A *How* solicitation focuses on getting students to talk through their process or report steps they followed to solve a problem. If a teacher is asking a student to list out multiple steps to a problem, or even just the next step, it would be considered a *How* question. Key words to look for in a *how* solicitation are *process, steps, method, procedure,* or *demonstrate.* We see some of these words show up in the following examples:

- "What did you do to get your answer?"
- "How did you get your answer?"
- "What was your process for solving the problem"
- "What should I do for the next step to solving the question?"

Again, we can see with the first example that even though the word *what* is in the example, the phrasing "What did you do" indicates a focus on process, which relates to *how.*

What. A *What* solicitation is focused on students providing facts or ideas without a justification or explaining a process. The most common type of *What* solicitation is just asking students for an answer. Another type of solicitation that is coded as *What* is simply asking students to read out part of a problem statement or recall something that was said earlier in a lesson. Key words to look out for a *what* solicitation are *what, answer, result,* or *solution.* We see these words in some of the following examples:

- "What did you get for number four?"
- "Can someone tell me what the answer is?"
- "What is the result when you plug the numbers into the equation?"
- "Do we have an example of where that's not true?"

Other. An *Other* solicitation is either a general solicitation focused on the content or a type of question that is focused not on content at all but on more logistic matters of the class. An *Other* type of solicitation doesn't necessarily require students to provide a new mathematical idea, but rather, it gives them other ways to share their thinking. A solicitation will often be coded as *Other* when a teacher is asking students if they have questions, how things are going, or generally asking for their thoughts. Here are a few examples of *Other* type solicitations:

- "Do you understand?," "Do you agree?," "Do you have any questions?"
- "What do we/you think?"
- "What comments do you have for the speaker?," "Is there anything you want to know more about?," "Do you want to add anything?"

- "Can someone repeat what Brenda just said?"
- "Is it possible to do that?"

Again, we see an example where the words "What did you think?" can still be an *Other* type question because it is just getting general ideas out rather than specifically asking for an answer.

The last question about repeating what Brenda said is coded as *Other* because the answer to the question is simply repeating what Brenda said, not offering any new ideas. In contrast, if a student was asked to "repeat what Brenda said *and* explain why," it would be coded as *Why* because it is asking for justification above and beyond restating Brenda's initial comment.

N/A. A teacher solicitation can be coded as *N/A* when there is no clear evidence of a recent teacher solicitation. Most often, this will happen when a student spontaneously makes a comment or asks a question when the teacher hasn't asked anything. For example, when students are responding directly to one another, this typically indicates that they are responding to each other's comments, not to a solicitation from the teacher. Nonetheless, just because a student wasn't called on, it doesn't mean that teacher solicitation is automatically N/A. For example, a teacher might ask, "What is the answer to this problem?" This is a *What* type question. Now, if a student simply shouted out the answer without being called on, we would still have an instance where a student was *not called on* but the solicitation was still *What* and not *N/A*.

Example one: Delayed solicitation. Suppose a teacher makes a solicitation such as "I want each group to explain how they got their answer to the homework problem." Ultimately, it could take ten to twenty minutes for all the groups to respond to this solicitation. Nonetheless, even if a lot of time had passed after the first solicitation, if students were still answering the same question, it would be coded as *How* rather than *N/A* because the students are clearly responding to the initial solicitation.

Student talk type

Summary description: *Student talk type* describes the type of statement that a student is making. This dimension follows the same categories as *teacher solicitation type*, except that student talk cannot be defined as *N/A* because student contributions are only coded when a student says something.

Dimension levels

1. Why—A student makes a statement explaining or justifying their thinking.
2. How—A student describes their solution method or their process.
3. What—A teacher provides an answer or recalls a fact.
4. Other—A teacher makes a non-content-related statement or asks a question.

Explanation and examples. The purpose of the student talk type dimension is to understand the nature of a student's statements during a given contribution. Because there may be multiple statements made in a single contribution, a coder has to determine at which level to code a student's contribution. This dimension is simpler to code than *teacher solicitation*, as there is only one criterion. If there are multiple statements in a single contribution, this dimension is coded according to the hierarchy of *Why* > *How* > *What* > *Other*. This hierarchy is in place to account for how a student responds when a teacher uses multiple questions with a single student to help elicit their reasoning in more depth.

When coding for student talk type, the coder does not distinguish between statements that are factually correct or incorrect. Similarly, the coder does not attend to the quality of a student's justification when coding a *Why* statement. Rather, it is simply the presence of a justification or not that would be the deciding factor.

It's noteworthy that student talk does not necessarily follow the same level as the teacher solicitation in the same contribution. This can happen for a variety of reasons. Often, if a teacher asks a *Why* question but hasn't established classroom norms of explanation, students may simply respond with answers or *What* statements. In the opposite situation, if a class has very strong norms for explanation, regardless of whether a teacher makes a general statement like "What do you think" (an *Other* statement) or "What is the answer?" (a *What* question), students may still respond by providing the answer *and* explaining their thinking (a *Why*-talk type). Because both teacher questions and student talk are coded to the highest level during a contribution, the particular statement that corresponds to the highest level of student talk may differ from the particular teacher question that was at the highest level.

Why. A *Why* statement occurs when a student explains or justifies their thinking about a particular answer, procedure, or concept. In a student statement, key words to look out for include *because*, *reason*, *why*, *my reasoning*, or *justification*. While the presence of any of these words does not guarantee that there is a

Why statement, they strongly suggest it. We see how these words play out in the following examples:

- "I don't think there is a real-valued solution *because* we have a negative in the square root."
- "The *reason* why I think this conjecture is false is that the example we found previously would work as a counterexample."
- "My *justification* for the problem is based in trial and error. After twenty-five attempts nothing worked, so I assume it is incorrect."

It's worth repeating that quality of a justification doesn't matter. The last example uses a proof by trial and error, which is not mathematically rigorous, but could still be a *Why* statement because it justifies the student's thinking.

How. A *How* statement occurs when a student talks through their process or reports steps they followed to solve a problem. This could be multiple steps or just a single step. Anytime a student simply recalls a procedure, it is a *How* statement. We define a procedure as a sequential or algorithmic list of discrete steps that a student follows (like a recipe). Key words to look for in a *How* statement are *what I did*, *how*, *process*, *steps*, *method*, *procedure*, or *first/next*. We see some of these words show up in the following examples:

- "*What I did* was move all of the *x*'s to one side and combine like terms."
- "My *process* involved completing the square."
- "The first *step* was to rationalize the denominator."
- "My *method* was ordinary least squares regression."

With the first example, even though the word *what* is in the example, the phrasing "what I did" indicates a focus on process, which relates to *how*.

What. A *What* statement occurs when a student provides facts or ideas without giving a justification or explaining a process. The most common type of *What* statement is just providing an answer. A *What* statement also takes place when a student reads out part of a problem statement. Key words to look out for A *what* statement are *I got*, *answer*, *result*, or *solution*. We see these words in some of the following examples:

- "*I got* fifteen."
- "My *answer* was seven."

- "My *result* was false."
- "My *solution* was a power series."
- "Five."

The last example, where the statement is a single word, is another common example of a *What* statement. When a student speaks only a few words it is commonly (but not always) a *What* statement.

Other. An *Other* statement occurs when a student either asks a question or makes a statement that is not a mathematical object, idea, statement, process, reasoning, or explanation. In general, a statement is coded as *Other* when a student makes a contribution but it doesn't fall neatly into any of the categories of *Why*, *How*, or *What*. Here are a few examples of *Other* type statements:

- A student says "Yes" or "No," indicating that they agree or disagree.
- "I agree."
- "I don't know."
- "Can you explain how you got the answer?"
- "What is the answer to number seven?"

Example one. A teacher asks a question, and a student responds, "Is the answer seven?" In this case, the student may actually be making a *What* statement even though it is framed as a question. Here, the student wants to say that the answer is seven but asks it as a question to distance themselves from the particular answer. That way, even if it is wrong, the student won't have to feel bad about not getting it right.

Student talk length

Summary description: Student talk length refers to the number of words in a single continuous utterance. Student talk length is *not* aggregated over multiple turns of talk in the same contribution.

Dimension levels

1. 1–4 words (a few words)
2. 5–20 words (~1 sentence)
3. 21+ words (~2+ sentences)

Explanation and examples. The purpose of student talk length is to understand to what extent students are able to express complete or extended thoughts in their own words. For this reason, talk is aggregated over a single statement rather than over multiple turns of talk because a long exchange back and forth could easily consist of many student words without having any elaborated statements.

The definition of this particular dimension may be altered depending on the use case for EQUIP. For example, in a real-time coding scenario, it is highly impractical to count words, so it is better to code for *a few words*, *one sentence*, or *multiple sentences*. When this coding scheme is used, even if a statement is a complete sentence, such as "I got five," this would be coded as *a few words* because it has four or fewer words. Thus, to be coded as *one sentence*, there should be a complete thought *and* five or more words.

In a research context, especially if there is a transcript of interactions, it is more accurate to use categories that count the actual number of words stated by students. This will allow for an unambiguous characterization. When using a more ambiguous scheme (*a few words* or *one sentence*), there may be some cases that are harder to determine, but usually these are rare and won't have a big impact on the overall data given back to a teacher for professional development.

When counting, it is important to have a standard way to count words and mathematical expressions. We offer the following guidelines:

- A single algebraic expression or equation is coded as a single word.
- Any word stated in isolation (outside of an expression) is coded as a single word, even if written in long-form (e.g., *fifty-seven* gets counted as one word, not two words).
- If a student states digits, and digits are relevant, they count as multiple words (e.g., if students are working on a permutations problem and they come up with "five-seven-six," it counts as three words and not one because they are talking about digits, not the number 576).

In some cases, it may not be possible to capture all the specifics of all of a student's speech because some words were indecipherable, inaudible, or not captured in a audio recording or transcript. In such a situation, the utterance is coded according to the best estimate of how many words were indecipherable (i.e., the indecipherable words still add to the length of talk).

If a student's speech is interrupted by side talk between a teacher and another student, the number of words are counted both before and after the side talk because the side talk is not part of the main classroom discourse and is just ignored.

Example one: A student makes multiple statements. Suppose a contribution consists of a student speaking 5 words, 25 words, and 10 words at 3 different times. In this case, the length of talk would be coded as 21+ words, the greatest length of talk in the sequence. This need not correspond with *student talk type* coded (i.e., 25 words could be a *What* statement, and 5 words is a *Why* statement; in this case, the talk would be coded as 21+ words and *Why*, the highest levels in each case).

Teacher evaluation

Summary description: If a teacher explicitly makes a judgment about the correctness or quality of a student statement, it is considered to be a teacher evaluation.

Dimension levels

1. Yes—The teacher explicitly evaluates a student idea.
2. No—The teacher does not explicitly evaluate a student idea.

Explanation and examples. The purpose of teacher evaluation is to see when a teacher is acting as the mathematical authority in the classroom or when the students have opportunities to act as authorities. Because this process can be subtle, we only code when a teacher explicitly makes a judgment about a student's ideas. In addition, if the teacher explicitly evaluates even a single student idea (e.g., when there are multiple student ideas), then it is coded as teacher evaluation. When coding for evaluations, we look for moments when the teacher makes positive or definite affirmations or criticisms of what a student says. We also look for moments when the teacher acts as the mathematical authority rather than allowing students to.

Yes. This dimension is coded as *Yes* when there is an explicit evaluation. We would code this when the teacher clearly says yes/no or right/wrong about a student idea. Key words to look for would include *yes, no, "This is correct," "That is not correct," "That's too high," right,* or *wrong.* If a teacher evaluates an idea and then asks for more information, that is also coded as an evaluation. The other case where we code *Yes* is when a teacher praises a student's idea. Key words to look for would include *good*, *great*, *good job*, *way to go*, or *nice*. This is different from thanking a student for participating, which instead focuses on the process and not the answer.

No. This dimension is coded as *No* if there is not a clear evaluation. Even an implicit evaluation (e.g., a teacher suggesting the response might not be correct but not saying it outright) would be coded as *No*. For example, a teacher could say *"I see," "Uh-huh," "Interesting,"* or *"Thanks for sharing"* and none of these would be coded as evaluations. Although the teacher is affirming the student, they are affirming the fact that they participated, not their response.

Notes

Preface

1. Pamela Newkirk, *Diversity, Inc.: The Failed Promise of a Billion-Dollar Business* (Bold Type Books, 2019).
2. Zhihui Fang, "A Review of Research on Teacher Beliefs and Practices," *Educational Research* 38, no. 1 (1996): 47–65, https://doi.org/10.1080/0013188960380104.
3. Edward H. Chang et al., "The Mixed Effects of Online Diversity Training," *Proceedings of the National Academy of Sciences* 116, no. 16 (2019): 7778–83, https://doi.org/10.1073/pnas.1816076116.
4. Self-report is suspect, especially when it comes to issues of equity, because of the "social desirability effect." People know the "right" things to say, whether or not they believe them. For example, in most contexts expressing overtly racist ideas would not be socially acceptable. Federico R. Waitoller and Alfredo J. Artiles, "A Decade of Professional Development Research for Inclusive Education: A Critical Review and Notes for a Research Program," *Review of Educational Research* 83, no. 3 (2013): 319–56, https://doi.org/10.3102/0034654313483905; Hillary Parkhouse et al., "Multicultural Education Professional Development: A Review of the Literature," *Review of Educational Research* 89, no. 3 (2019): 416–58, https://doi.org/10.3102/0034654319840359; Andrew Matschiner, "A Systematic Review of the Literature on Inservice Professional Development Explicitly Addressing Race and Racism," *Review of Educational Research* 93, no. 4 (2022): 594–630, https://doi.org/10.3102/00346543221125245.
5. Paola Sztajn et al., "Research on Mathematics Professional Development," in *The Compendium for Research in Mathematics Education*, ed. Jinja Cai (National Council of Teachers of Mathematics, 2017).

Introduction

1. There is also backlash. In the US, this has played out with antidiversity legislation, such as ending affirmation action, banning critical race theory from schools, and overturning *Roe v. Wade*. In local political climates that are hostile toward diversity, there are additional challenges to taking up the ideas in this book.
2. Elaine Seymour and Nancy M. Hewitt, *Talking About Leaving: Why Undergraduates Leave the Sciences* (Westview Press, 1997).
3. Daniel L. Reinholz et al., "Evaluating Scholarly Teaching: A Model and Call for an Evidence-Based Approach," in *Learning Analytics in Higher Education: Current Innovations, Future Potential, and Practical Applications*, ed. J. Lester et al. (Routledge, 2019), 69–92.
4. Michael S. Garet et al., "What Makes Professional Development Effective? Results from a National Sample of Teachers," *American Educational Research Journal* 38, no. 4 (2001): 915–45.
5. Conference Board of the Mathematical Sciences, "Active Learning in Post-Secondary Mathematics Education" (Washington, DC: Conference Board of the Mathematical Sciences, 2016), http://www.cbmsweb.org/Statements/Active_Learning_Statement.pdf.

6. J. Bransford, "Technology to Support Learning," chap. 9 in *How People Learn: Brain, Mind, Experience, and School* (National Academies Press, 2000); John Dunlosky et al., "Improving Students' Learning with Effective Learning Techniques: Promising Directions from Cognitive and Educational Psychology," *Psychological Science in the Public Interest* 14, no. 1 (2013): 4–58, https://doi.org/10.1177/1529100612453266.
7. John Dewey, *How We Think: A Restatement of the Relation of Reflective Thinking to the Educative Process* (D. C. Heath and Company, 1933).
8. Norm Friesen, "The Lecture as a Transmedial Pedagogical Form: A Historical Analysis," *Educational Researcher* 40, no. 3 (2011): 95–102, https://doi.org/10.3102/0013189X11404603.
9. Daniel Z. Grunspan et al., "The Lecture Machine: A Cultural Evolutionary Model of Pedagogy in Higher Education," *CBE—Life Sciences Education* 17, no. 3 (2018): es6, https://doi.org/10.1187/cbe.17–12–0287.
10. Seymour and Hewitt, *Talking About Leaving*; H. Thiry et al., *Talking About Leaving Revisited: Persistence, Relocation, and Loss in Undergraduate STEM Education*, ed. Elaine Seymour and Anne-Barrie Hunter (Springer, 2019).
11. A. H. Schoenfeld, "The Math Wars," *Educational Policy* 18, no. 1 (2004): 253–86, https://doi.org/10.1177/0895904803260042.
12. J. Wai, "Why Is It Socially Acceptable to Be Bad at Math?," *Psychology Today*, March 25, 2012, http://www.psychologytoday.com/blog/finding-the-next-einstein/201203/why-is-it-socially-acceptable-be-bad-math.
13. Ina V. S. Mullis et al., "TIMSS 2019 International Results in Mathematics and Science," Boston College, TIMSS & PIRLS International Study Center, 2020, https://www.skolporten.se/app/uploads/2020/12/timss-2019-highlights-1.pdf; Eric A. Hanushek et al., *U.S. Math Performance in Global Perspective* (2010).
14. President's Council of Advisors on Science and Technology, *Engage to Excel: Producing One Million Additional College Graduates with Degrees in Science, Technology, Engineering, and Mathematics*, February 2012.
15. Conference Board, "Active Learning"
16. Na'ilah Suad Nasir et al., "Rethinking Learning: What the Interdisciplinary Science Tells Us," *Educational Researcher* 50, no. 8 (2021): 557–65, https://doi.org/10.3102/0013189X211047251.
17. Andrea Bender and Sieghard Beller, "Fingers as a Tool for Counting—Naturally Fixed or Culturally Flexible?," *Frontiers in Psychology* 2 (October, 2011): 256, https://doi.org/10.3389/fpsyg.2011.00256; Andrea Bender and Sieghard Beller, "Nature and Culture of Finger Counting: Diversity and Representational Effects of an Embodied Cognitive Tool," *Cognition* 124, no. 2 (2012): 156–82, https://doi.org/10.1016/j.cognition.2012.05.005.
18. Jian Weng et al., "The Effects of Long-Term Abacus Training on Topological Properties of Brain Functional Networks," *Scientific Reports* 7, no. 1 (2017): 8862, https://doi.org/10.1038/s41598–017–08955–2.
19. Cesar Delgado, "Cross-Cultural Study of Understanding of Scale and Measurement: Does the Everyday Use of US Customary Units Disadvantage US Students?," *International Journal of Science Education* 35, no. 8 (2013): 1277–98, https://doi.org/10.1080/09500693.2013.779761.
20. Marilyn M. Vihman, "Learning Words and Learning Sounds: Advances in Language Development," *British Journal of Psychology* 108, no. 1 (2017): 1–27, https://doi.org/10.1111/bjop.12207.

21. Daniel L. Everett, "What Does Pirahã Grammar Have to Teach Us About Human Language and the Mind?," *WIREs Cognitive Science* 3, no. 6 (2012): 555–63, https://doi.org/10.1002/wcs.1195; Martin Maier and Rasha Abdel Rahman, "Native Language Promotes Access to Visual Consciousness," *Psychological Science* 29, no. 11 (2018): 1757–72, https://doi.org/10.1177/0956797618782181.
22. Jasone Cenoz, "The Influence of Bilingualism on Third Language Acquisition: Focus on Multilingualism," *Language Teaching* 46, no. 1 (2013): 71–86, https://doi.org/10.1017/S0261444811000218.
23. Gottfried Schlaug et al., "Effects of Music Training on the Child's Brain and Cognitive Development," *Annals of the New York Academy of Sciences* 1060, no. 1 (2005): 219–30, https://doi.org/10.1196/annals.1360.015; Sofia Seinfeld et al., "Effects of Music Learning and Piano Practice on Cognitive Function, Mood and Quality of Life in Older Adults," *Frontiers in Psychology* 4 (2013), https://www.frontiersin.org/journals/psychology/articles/10.3389/fpsyg.2013.00810.
24. L. S. Vygotsky, *Mind in Society: The Development of Higher Mental Process* (Harvard University Press, 1978); J. Lave and E. Wenger, *Communities of Practice* (Cambridge University Press, 1998).
25. Allison R. Firestone et al., "Teacher Study Groups: An Integrative Literature Synthesis," *Review of Educational Research* 90, no. 5 (2020): 675–709, https://doi.org/10.3102/0034654320938128; Mary M. Kennedy, "How Does Professional Development Improve Teaching?," *Review of Educational Research* 86, no. 4 (2016): 945–80, https://doi.org/10.3102/0034654315626800.
26. Hilda Borko, "Professional Development and Teacher Learning: Mapping the Terrain," *Educational Researcher* 33, no. 8 (2004): 3–15, https://doi.org/10.3102/0013189X033008003.
27. Inken Gast et al., "Team-Based Professional Development Interventions in Higher Education: A Systematic Review," *Review of Educational Research* 87, no. 4 (2017): 736–67, https://doi.org/10.3102/0034654317704306; Susan Thomas et al., "A Qualitative Review of Literature on Peer Review of Teaching in Higher Education: An Application of the SWOT Framework," *Review of Educational Research* 84, no. 1 (2014): 112–59, https://doi.org/10.3102/0034654313499617; Cheryl Amundsen and Mary Wilson, "Are We Asking the Right Questions?: A Conceptual Review of the Educational Development Literature in Higher Education," *Review of Educational Research* 82, no. 1 (2012): 90–126, https://doi.org/10.3102/0034654312438409.
28. Garet et al., "Professional Development"; V. Darleen Opfer and David Pedder, "Conceptualizing Teacher Professional Learning," *Review of Educational Research* 81, no. 3 (2011): 376–407, https://doi.org/10.3102/0034654311413609.
29. Laura M. Desimone and Katie Pak, "Instructional Coaching as High-Quality Professional Development," *Theory Into Practice* 56, no. 1 (2017): 3–12, https://doi.org/10.1080/00405841.2016.1241947.
30. Lave and Wenger, *Communities of Practice.*
31. J. Lave and E. Wenger, *Situated Learning: Legitimate Peripheral Participation* (Cambridge University Press, 1991).
32. Austin S. Jennings and Amanda Jennings, "Comprehensive and Superficial Data Users: A Convergent Mixed Methods Study of Teachers' Practice of Interim Assessment Data Use," *Teachers College Record* 122, no. 12 (2020): 1–46, https://doi.org/10.1177/016146812012201210.

33. Julie A. Marsh et al., "Using Data to Alter Instructional Practice: The Mediating Role of Coaches and Professional Learning Communities," *Teachers College Record* 117, no. 4 (2015): 1–40, https://doi.org/10.1177/016146811511700411.
34. Elizabeth N. Farley-Ripple and Joan L. Buttram, "Developing Collaborative Data Use Through Professional Learning Communities: Early Lessons from Delaware," *Studies in Educational Evaluation* 42 (September 2014): 41–53, https://doi.org/10.1016/j.stueduc.2013.09.006.
35. Neal A. Raisman, The Educational Policy Institute, *The Cost of College Attrition at Four-Year Colleges & Universities*, February 2013.
36. Furthermore, as instructors make concrete progress on local equity issues, it better positions them to contribute to equity efforts more broadly. For example, many of the instructors in this book engaged in broader equity work after they completed time in an equity learning community (e.g., running equity workshops for peers).
37. N. Shah and C. M. Lewis, "Amplifying and Attenuating Inequity in Collaborative Learning: Toward an Analytical Framework," *Cognition and Instruction* 37, no. 4 (2019): 1–30, https://doi.org/10.1080/07370008.2019.1631825.
38. Marsha Ing et al., "Student Participation in Elementary Mathematics Classrooms: The Missing Link Between Teacher Practices and Student Achievement?," *Educational Studies in Mathematics* 90, no. 3 (2015): 341–56; D. L. Reinholz et al., "When Active Learning Is Inequitable: Women's Participation Predicts Gender Inequities in Mathematical Performance," *Journal for Research in Mathematics Education* 53, no. 3 (2022): 204–26, https://doi.org/10.5951/jresematheduc-2020–0143; Margaret Walshaw and Glenda Anthony, "The Teacher's Role in Classroom Discourse: A Review of Recent Research Into Mathematics Classrooms," *Review of Educational Research* 78, no. 3 (2008): 516–51, https://doi.org/10.3102/0034654308320292.
39. Dunlosky et al., "Improving Students' Learning."
40. Benedikt Wisniewski et al., "The Power of Feedback Revisited: A Meta-Analysis of Educational Feedback Research," *Frontiers in Psychology* 10 (2020), https://www.frontiersin.org/articles/10.3389/fpsyg.2019.03087.
41. Na'ilah Suad Nasir, "Identity, Goals, and Learning: Mathematics in Cultural Practice," *Mathematical Thinking and Learning* 4, no. 2–3 (2002): 213–47, https://doi.org/10.1207/S15327833MTL04023_6.
42. Daniel L. Reinholz et al., "Active Learning"; Daniel L. Reinholz and Anne G. Wilhelm, "Race-Gender D/Discourses in Mathematics Education: (Re)-Producing Inequitable Participation Patterns Across a Diverse, Instructionally-Advanced Urban District," *Urban Education* 49, no.8 (2022): 1–31, https://doi.org/10.1177/00420859221107614.
43. Rosangela Bando et al., "Effect of Inquiry and Problem Based Pedagogy on Learning: Evidence from 10 Field Experiments in Four Countries," Working Paper (National Bureau of Economic Research, September 2019), https://doi.org/10.3386/w26280.
44. W. G. Secada, "Educational Equity Versus Equality of Education: An Alternative Conception," in *Equity in Education*, ed. W. G. Secada (Falmer, 1989), 68–88.
45. Reinholz and Wilhelm, "Race-Gender D/Discourses."
46. For example, Daniel L. Reinholz et al., "Moving Beyond Gatekeeping: Using Data Analytics to Overcome Resistance to Pedagogical Change," in *Proceedings of CERME 12* (2022); Reinholz et al., "Active Learning"; Daniel L. Reinholz et al., "A Pandemic Crash Course: Learning to Teach Equitably in Synchronous Online Classes," *CBE—Life Sciences Education* 19, no. 4 (2020): ar60, https://doi.org/10.1187/cbe.20–06–0126; N. Shah et al.,

"Racial Hierarchy and Masculine Space: Participatory In/Equity in Computational Physics Classrooms," *Computer Science Education* 30, no. 3 (2020): 1–25, https://doi.org/10.1080/08993408.2020.1805285.

47. For example, Katelyn M. Cooper and Sara E. Brownell, "Coming Out in Class: Challenges and Benefits of Active Learning in a Biology Classroom for LGBTQIA Students," *CBE—Life Sciences Education* 15, no. 3 (2016): ar37, https://doi.org/10.1187/cbe.16–01–0074; Jessica Brooke Ernest et al., "Hidden Competence: Women's Mathematical Participation in Public and Private Classroom Spaces," *Educational Studies in Mathematics* 102, 2019, https://doi.org/10.1007/s10649–019–09910-w; Carola Suárez-Orozco et al., "Toxic Rain in Class: Classroom Interpersonal Microaggressions," *Educational Researcher* 44, no. 3 (2015): 151–60, https://doi.org/10.3102/0013189X15580314.
48. D. B. Martin, "Learning Mathematics While Black," *Educational Foundations* 26, no. 1–2 (2012): 47–66; Joseph P. Robinson-Cimpian et al., "Teachers' Perceptions of Students' Mathematics Proficiency May Exacerbate Early Gender Gaps in Achievement," *Developmental Psychology* 50, no. 4 (2014): 1262–81, https://doi.org/10.1037/a0035073.
49. Hannah-Hanh D. Nguyen and Ann Marie Ryan, "Does Stereotype Threat Affect Test Performance of Minorities and Women? A Meta-Analysis of Experimental Evidence," *Journal of Applied Psychology* 93, no. 6 (2008): 1314–34, https://doi.org/10.1037/a0012702; S. J. Spencer et al., "Stereotype Threat," *Annual Review of Psychology* 67, no. 1 (2016): 415–37, https://doi.org/10.1146/annurev-psych-073115–103235.
50. Prudence L. Carter et al., "You Can't Fix What You Don't Look At: Acknowledging Race in Addressing Racial Discipline Disparities," *Urban Education* 52, no. 2 (2017): 207–35, https://doi.org/10.1177/0042085916660350.
51. R. A. Lotan, "Equitable Classrooms: A Compelling Connection Between Theory and Practice," in *Unequals*, ed. M. Webster and L. S. Walker (Oxford University Press, 2022), 178–99, https://doi.org/10.1093/oso/9780197600009.003.0009; E. G. Cohen and R. A. Lotan, *Working for Equity in Heterogeneous Classrooms: Sociological Theory into Practice* (Teachers College Press, 1997).
52. D. Sadker et al., *Still Failing at Fairness: How Gender Bias Cheats Girls and Boys in School and What We Can Do about It* (Simon and Schuster, 2009).
53. Reinholz and Wilhelm, "Race-Gender D/Discourses."
54. We could not explore the experiences of gender nonbinary students given that this study was a secondary analysis of existing data and the initial data were collected using a binary lens.
55. Despite racial inequities, the relatively high levels of participation from Black students (in this study) were a positive finding. To understand those results, we performed a discourse analysis and analyzed the perspectives and approaches of district leaders. From this analysis, it was clear that the district had been engaging in long-term, productive, systemic professional development to mitigate inequities for Black learners. Additionally, the leaders paid little to no attention to gender as a focal area of inequity. To summarize, gender and racial inequities were apparent across the district, and these inequities could be connected to discourses that were present in the district. This study provides observational evidence that patterns of participation are malleable, with intentional focus; The Asian populations in this study were primarily from Hmong refugee communities. It is important to recognize that Asians are not monolithic and different groups have different experiences despite an overarching narrative that all Asians are successful at mathematics all the time; An important caveat is that these studies did not necessarily have statistical power to investigate inequities across all racialized groups in each setting. For example, we found evidence of considerable

marginalization of Native students in this study, but we couldn't explore it statistically due to small sample sizes.

56. Ernest et al., "Hidden Competence"; Reinholz et al., "Crash Course"; Daniel L. Reinholz et al., "Walking the Walk: Using Classroom Analytics to Support Instructors to Address Implicit Bias in Teaching," *International Journal for Academic Development* 25, no. 3 (2020): 259–72, https://doi.org/10.1080/1360144X.2019.1692211; Daniel L. Reinholz and N. Shah, "Equity Analytics: A Methodological Approach for Quantifying Participation Patterns in Mathematics Classroom Discourse," *Journal for Research in Mathematics Education* 49, no. 2 (2018): 140–77; Shah et al., "Racial Hierarchy"; N. Shah et al., "Why Mrs. Stone Never Calls on Debra: A Case of Race-Gender Ideology in Practice," in *The Interdisciplinarity of the Learning Sciences, 14th International Conference of the Learning Sciences (ICLS) 2020,* ed. M. Gresalfi and I. S. Horn, vol. 1 (International Society of the Learning Sciences, 2020), 1974–81; N. Shah and S. Crespo, "Cultural Narratives and Status Hierarchies," in *Mathematical Discourse That Breaks Barriers and Creates Space for Marginalized Learners,* ed. R. Hunter et al. (Sense Publishers, 2017), 23–38.
57. Daniel L. Reinholz et al., "Utilizing Data Analytics to Incorporate Racial Equity into STEM Faculty Development," in *Handbook of STEM Faculty Development* (2022), ed. Sandra M. Linder, Information Age Publishing.; Reinholz et al., "Crash Course"; Shah et al., "Racial Hierarchy."
58. Sadker et al., *Failing at Fairness.*
59. Reinholz et al., "A Pandemic Crash Course"; Reinholz et al., "Utilizing Data Analytics"; Reinholz et al., "Walking the Walk"; Reinholz and Shah, "Equity Analytics"; Shah et al., "Racial Hierarchy."
60. Participant patterns generally align with forms of privilege. For example, the lived experiences of an economically privileged Asian American who has been in the US for generations is vastly different from a recent refugee and emergent multilingual student. Clearly, categories such as "Asian" are oversimplifications that may obscure important within-group differences. At the same time, these racial-category markers do matter and can be used as a tool for positive change.
61. C. Yeh et al., "Beyond Verbal: A Methodological Approach for Capturing Multimodal Engagement in Mathematics Classrooms," *Educational Researcher*, n.d., https://doi.org/10.3102/0013189X241310169.
62. To be fair, I have also had my own teaching coded on multiple occasions, and despite being a researcher who studies inequities, forms of inequity were still present!
63. Ernest et al., "Hidden Competence"; Shah et al., "Racial Hierarchy"; Because the six case studies below focus on whole-class instruction, I won't spend much time on those studies here.
64. Garet et al., "Professional Development."

Chapter 1

1. Daniel L. Reinholz et al., "When Active Learning Is Inequitable: Women's Participation Predicts Gender Inequities in Mathematical Performance," *Journal for Research in Mathematics Education* 53, no. 3 (2022): 204–26, https://doi.org/10.5951/jresematheduc-2020-0143; Daniel L. Reinholz and N. Shah, "Equity Analytics: A Methodological Approach for Quantifying Participation Patterns in Mathematics Classroom Discourse," *Journal for Research in Mathematics Education* 49, no. 2 (2018): 140–77; Daniel L. Reinholz and Anne G. Wilhelm, "Race-Gender D/Discourses in Mathematics Education:

(Re)-Producing Inequitable Participation Patterns Across a Diverse, Instructionally-Advanced Urban District," *Urban Education* 49, no.8 (2022): 1–31, https://doi.org/10.1177/00420859221107614.

2. Reinholz and Shah, "Equity Analytics."
3. For example, M. D. Boston, "Assessing Instructional Quality in Mathematics," *The Elementary School Journal* 113, no. 1 (2012): 76–104, https://doi.org/10.1086/666387; Michelle K. Smith et al., "The Classroom Observation Protocol for Undergraduate STEM (COPUS): A New Instrument to Characterize University STEM Classroom Practices," *CBE—Life Sciences Education* 12, no. 4 (2013): 618–27, https://doi.org/10.1187/cbe.13-08-0154.
4. Daniel L. Reinholz et al., "A Pandemic Crash Course: Learning to Teach Equitably in Synchronous Online Classes," *CBE—Life Sciences Education* 19, no. 4 (2020): ar60, https://doi.org/10.1187/cbe.20-06-0126; Daniel L. Reinholz et al., "Walking the Walk: Using Classroom Analytics to Support Instructors to Address Implicit Bias in Teaching," *International Journal for Academic Development* 25, no. 3 (2020): 259–72, https://doi.org/10.1080/1360144X.2019.1692211; N. Shah et al., "Racial Hierarchy and Masculine Space: Participatory In/Equity in Computational Physics Classrooms," *Computer Science Education* 30, no. 3 (2020): 1–25, https://doi.org/10.1080/08993408.2020.1805285. In contrast, in our society, it is much easier for people to talk about gender and gender inequities, at least in a binary way.
5. This connects directly to the idea of color blindness (saying that all students are the same or one does not see race). In White American culture, many of us were raised to believe that color blindness is a good thing, so it's not surprising that this is a default stance many instructors take.
6. We have chosen to define contributions in this way to allow for back-and-forth between a single student and the instructor. For example, during a verbal discussion, if a teacher were to ask follow-up questions to a single student to probe deeper into their thinking, it would all be considered part of a single contribution. This allows us to account for *teacher press*—when an instructor asks follow-up questions to the same student—to capture the highest-level forms of engagement present. It would be equally valid to define contributions differently, and it would be an empirical question whether another definition was more or less conducive to changing practice.
7. R. A. Lotan, "Equitable Classrooms: A Compelling Connection Between Theory and Practice," in *Unequals*, ed. M. Webster and L. S. Walker (Oxford University Press, 2022), 178–99, https://doi.org/10.1093/oso/9780197600009.003.0009; Na'ilah Suad Nasir et al., "Rethinking Learning: What the Interdisciplinary Science Tells Us," *Educational Researcher* 50, no. 8 (2021): 557–65, https://doi.org/10.3102/0013189X211047251.
8. If resources allow for it, a camera operator can capture higher-fidelity videos and pan between the instructor and students. This can also be achieved with multiple cameras placed strategically.
9. When capturing small-group interactions, a decision must be made whether to focus a camera on a single group for the duration of observation, whether to move it between groups at a set time interval, or to follow the instructor throughout the lesson. Each choice is valid but will support different inferences based on the instructor's goals. If multiple cameras are available, it is possible to capture a few of the groups simultaneously; Jessica Brooke Ernest et al., "Hidden Competence: Women's Mathematical Participation in Public and Private Classroom Spaces," *Educational Studies in Mathematics*, 102 (2019), https://doi.org/10.1007/s10649-019-09910-w. With Zoom, the cloud recording is especially useful because it

captures transcripts of the conversation and identifies speakers; Reinholz et al., "A Pandemic Crash Course"; Liza Bondurant and Daniel L. Reinholz, "'Rahul Is a Math Nerd' and 'Mia Can Be a Drama Queen': How Mixed-Reality Simulations Can Perpetuate Racist and Sexist Stereotypes," *Mathematics Teacher Educator* 11, no. 3 (2023): 189–209, https://doi.org/10.5951/MTE.2021–0041.

10. C. Yeh, D. L. Reinholz, H. H. Lee, and M. G. Moschetti, "Beyond Verbal: A Methodological Approach for Capturing Multimodal Engagement in Mathematics Classrooms," *Educational Researcher* (2025), https://doi.org/10.3102/0013189X241310169.
11. Reinholz and Shah, "Equity Analytics."
12. In previous work, we used another metric called the *equity ratio*. A ratio of one indicated proportional participation relative to group size, greater than one was disproportionately high participation, and less than one was disproportionately low participation. Yet our empirical work showed that this ratio could be difficult for instructors to interpret and, worse, could lead to negative unintended consequences, so we have stopped using this metric in our work. This example highlights that not all data are equally useful and more data is not always better.
13. William R. Penuel et al., "Belonging in Science Classrooms: Investigating Its Relation to Students' Contributions and Influence in Knowledge Building," *Journal of Research in Science Teaching* 61, no. 1 (2024): 228–52, https://doi.org/10.1002/tea.21884.
14. We have built such learning communities in a variety of settings (e.g., K–12 schools, community colleges) and configurations (e.g., instructors coding themselves). We have also used multiple lead coaches at the same time working together.
15. As the lead researcher responsible for studying the cases in this book, I conducted interviews with faculty participants and provided notes from the interviews to the coaches.
16. The full interview protocol can be found in the appendix on methodology.
17. Practically, this is most common in K–12 settings where student information is directly available to teachers. In higher education, we find more often than not that instructors do not have direct access to student information and gathering it from the university can be a challenge.
18. Real-time coding may be less accurate; simplifying the coding scheme (i.e., one to two dimensions) helps ensure accuracy for real-time observations.
19. As noted earlier, two participants, Kelly and Elayne, were the only instructors in their learning communities. Still, the community of coach, student coder, and single instructor still provided productive space for community building.
20. In capitalism, functionally, all human contexts have hierarchies (even in organizations that aim to be "flat"), or at least I've yet to study or experience a context that doesn't.
21. To be clear, our hypothesis is not always correct, and we may go back and change our social markers of focus later.
22. In homogeneous contexts, we may not include race or gender. For example, I've worked with an instructor in a women's college (all cisgender women) and a community college instructor serving Latine communities (over 90 percent of the students). In that context, rather than looking at racial and ethnic categories, it made sense to look at more nuanced aspects of Latine identity (e.g., language, country of origin, newcomer status).
23. Courtney Ngai et al., *Facilitating Change in Higher Education: The Departmental Action Team Model* (Glitter Cannon Press, 2020).
24. Daniel L. Reinholz, *Equitable and Engaging Mathematics Teaching: A Guide to Disrupting Hierarchies in the Classroom*, MAA Notes 97 (MAA Press, 2023).

25. Focusing on commonalities across instructors is a productive way to do this.
26. One complexity with microaggressions is that different minoritized individuals may experience them differently. Nevertheless, there are commonly understood microaggressions, and it is important to use care around those specific topics.

Chapter 2

1. E. G. Cohen and R. A. Lotan, *Designing Groupwork: Strategies for the Heterogeneous Classroom*, 3rd ed. (Teachers College Press, 2014).

Chapter 3

1. Luca and Akira were also half Asian, and Elia was half Black.

Chapter 4

1. During his participation in the learning community, five observations of Sam's teaching were coded. However, because he was teaching virtually, he recorded additional lessons. These were later analyzed to verify that in four baseline lessons (all taking place before Observation 2), Sarah only participated in class one time.

Chapter 5

1. Daniel L. Reinholz, *Equitable and Engaging Mathematics Teaching: A Guide to Disrupting Hierarchies in the Classroom*, MAA Notes 97 (MAA Press, 2023).
2. Stan Yoshinobu, "Letter: Dear Student," *The IBL Blog*, September 4, 2019, http://theiblblog.blogspot.com/2019/09/letter-dear-student.html.

Chapter 6

1. Daniel L. Reinholz, *Equitable and Engaging Mathematics Teaching: A Guide to Disrupting Hierarchies in the Classroom*, MAA Notes 97 (MAA Press, 2023).

Appendix A

1. In prior settings, we used face-to-face debrief meetings, but given the COVID-19 pandemic and the remote location of the participants, we used virtual debriefs.
2. Hugh Mehan, "'What Time Is It, Denise?': Asking Known Information Questions in Classroom Discourse," *Theory into Practice* 18, no. 4 (1979): 285–94.
3. Maureen P. Boyd and Donald L. Rubin, "Elaborated Student Talk in an Elementary ESoL Classroom," *Research in the Teaching of English* 36, no. 4 (2002): 495–530.
4. M. T. H. Chi et al., "Eliciting Self-Explanations Improves Understanding," *Cognitive Science* 18, no. 3 (1994): 439–77, https://doi.org/10.1016/0364–0213(94)90016–7; T. Lombrozo, "The Structure and Function of Explanations," *Trends in Cognitive Sciences* 10, no. 10 (2006): 464–70, https://doi.org/doi:10.1016/j.tics.2006.08.004.
5. M. Braaten and M. Windschitl, "Working Toward a Stronger Conceptualization of Scientific Explanation for Science Education," *Science Education* 95, no. 4 (2011): 639–69; Marjorie Henningsen and Mary Kay Stein, "Mathematical Tasks and Student Cognition: Classroom-Based Factors That Support and Inhibit High-Level Mathematical Thinking and Reasoning," *Journal for Research in Mathematics Education* 28, no. 5 (1997): 524–49.
6. S. Michaels et al., "Accountable Talk Sourcebook" (Institute for Learning, 2010).

7. R. A. Engle, "The Productive Disciplinary Engagement Framework: Origins, Key Concepts, and Developments," in *Design Research on Learning and Thinking in Educational Settings: Enhancing Intellectual Growth and Functioning*, ed. D. Yun Dai (Routledge, 2012), 170–209.

Appendix B

1. M. K. Stein, R. A. Engle, M. S. Smith, and E. K. Hughes, "Orchestrating Productive Mathematical Discussions: Five Practices for Helping Teachers Move beyond Show and Tell," *Mathematical Thinking and Learning* 10, no. 4 (2008): 313–40, https://doi.org/10.1080/10986060802229675.

About the Author

Daniel L. Reinholz is a professor in the Department of Mathematics and Statistics at San Diego State University. Broadly speaking, his research focuses on creating tools for educational transformation, to improve equity and mitigate systemic oppression. Reinholz codeveloped the EQUIP tool, which is a free web-based classroom observational tool for tracking patterns of student participation for different student groups. He has become a foremost expert in equitable teaching strategies for postsecondary mathematics and STEM. Ultimately, the goal of his work is to change the education system so that it can be more just and better serve the needs of all students. This work includes running sophisticated professional development that goes well beyond equity talk to produce lasting changes to practices and institutions.

Reinholz served as a postdoctoral fellow in the Center for STEM Learning at the University of Colorado Boulder and received a PhD from the University of California, Berkeley.

Index